U.S. ARMY CHEVROLET TRUCKS IN WORLD WAR II

1½-ton, 4x4

CASEMATE | ILLUSTRATED | SPECIAL

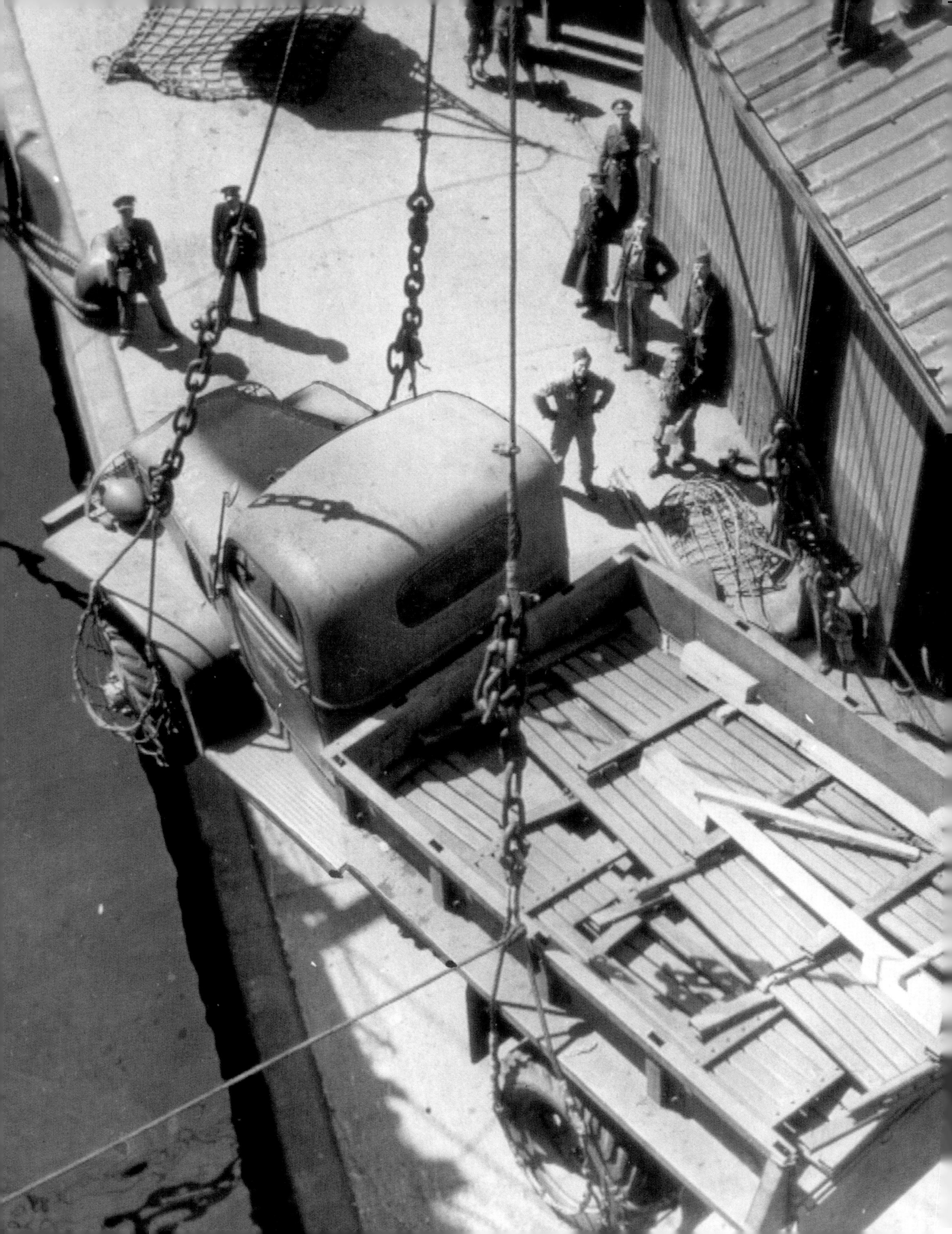

CASEMATE | ILLUSTRATED | SPECIAL

U.S. ARMY CHEVROLET TRUCKS IN WORLD WAR II

1½-ton, 4x4

DIDIER ANDRES

Acknowledgements

For their unwavering help and support, I would like to give special thanks to Alexandre Delbes, without whom all the documents assembled would never have come together; to Michel Roques, an old friend, tireless reader of my drafts and supplier of highly relevant historical points; to Thierry Mahot for his images and his renovation work, which allowed me to discover many peculiarities of these small trucks; and to Joann Borsato for her pertinent feedback and comments.

To you Guy Decerf, without our many debates on the subject, this book would certainly not have seen the light of day; we miss you.

Thank you to the TM-WWII PDF Military Manuals company for its availability and access to its documents. http://www.tm-ww2.com/

CISS0003

Published in the United States of America and Great Britain in 2020 by

CASEMATE PUBLISHERS
1950 Lawrence Road, Havertown, PA 19083, USA
and
The Old Music Hall, 106–108 Cowley Road, Oxford OX4 1JE, UK

This book is published in cooperation with, and under license from, Sophie Histoire & Collections. Originally published in French as *Les Camions Chevrolets 4x4 de l'US Army* © Histoire & Collections 2018

Hardback Edition: ISBN 978-1-61200-8639
Digital Edition: ISBN 978-1-61200-8646

A CIP record for this book is available from the British Library

Design by Myriam Bell
Translated by Myriam Bell
Printed and bound in the Czech Republic by FINIDR s.r.o.

For a complete list of Casemate titles, please contact:
CASEMATE PUBLISHERS (US)
Telephone (610) 853-9131
Fax (610) 853-9146
Email: casemate@casematepublishers.com
www.casematepublishers.com

CASEMATE PUBLISHERS (UK)
Telephone (01865) 241249
Email: casemate-uk@casematepublishers.co.uk
www.casematepublishers.co.uk

Title page: These two winchless Chevy cargo dump YP-G-4112-YHs test the strength of a bridge during exercises in the U.S. (U.S. Army SC-120006)

Contents

1 Introduction

Between 1940 and 1945, the Chevrolet Motor Division of General Motors Corporation delivered, all categories included, over 170,000 vehicles to the U.S. Army.

The Chevrolet 1½-ton, 4x4 prototype. The main visual characteristics are its Studebaker-like flat wings and the winch under the bumper, the latter being typical of the G-4412 series. (U.S. Army)

Within this production run—which does not take into account prototypes and pre-series models—157,907 units were 1½-ton, 4x4s. However, the classification system used by Chevrolet is complex and deserves a closer look.

The relationship between Chevrolet and the U.S. Army goes back much further than the beginning of World War II. This firm in Detroit, Michigan, had delivered numerous vehicles to the Army in the 1930s. When, in 1939, the Quartermaster Corps was obliged to standardize the various categories of vehicles according to their payload by using only five classes (½-, 1½-, 2½-, 4-, and 7½-ton), many manufacturers answered the call for tender. In contrast, Chevrolet remained quiet and lost the first few orders of 1½-ton payload trucks, which should have been their strong suit. It was Dodge that delivered the first vehicles in this category, with its VF series.

During the second half of the 1940s, Chevrolet returned to the forefront of the scene, producing a vehicle with resolutely modern lines. It left behind the competition's rounded forms, to present a prototype with strict lines, directly inspired by the new CCKWX-353 of its parent firm, the Yellow Truck & Coach Manufacturing Company. Moreover, from the outset the new Chevy benefited from mechanical elements—specifically axles—common in other General Motors products. The company was innovative with the famous Banjo axles and was thus able to make do without the Timken-Detroit Company and its Split axles.

Often Chevrolets are confused with CCKW(X)s, because the two vehicles were built by entities within the same group. It is easy to imagine then that the resemblance was a marketing ploy, the results of which were manifested in the cabin's lines and also

At the Service Corps depot at Fort Holabird, Baltimore. The low exhaust outlet in front of the mudguard is also a characteristic of the earlier vehicles. (U.S. Army)

in internal details. In fact, in 1940/1, everything was different: the means by which the cabin was affixed to the chassis, the axles which had nothing in common, and the differences that could be noted even down to the nuts and bolts. It wasn't until 1942 that a semblance of familiarity between the two parent companies became apparent. When orders for the CCKW reached maximum production levels for the Split axles, a solution had to be found: Banjo axles on Chevrolet 4x4s became the answer to General Motors' 6x6s.

April 1940 at the Holabird Research Center's test track. This photo was taken during the prototype's evaluation in front of officers.

Production

Three major series succeeded each other on the production line:

From November 1940 to April 1941, the first productions were classified as YP (short wheelbase) and YQ (long wheelbase), both included either in the G-4112 or the G-4013 reference, with no further distinction in their function. These amounted to 11,212 vehicles, representing around 7 percent of the 1½-ton, 4x4 production. They were directly issued from pre-series models.

From April to September 1941, with new administrative definitions, the second generation saw significant structural modifications take place, ZP (short wheelbase) and ZQ (long wheelbase), both included in references G-4163, 4174, 4152, 4105, 4165, 4113, and 4162, which defined the particular function of the vehicles. 8,924 trucks were produced, around 6 percent of the production run.

From September 1941 to the end of production, 138,771 Chevrolets (around 87 percent of the production run) were designed as series G-7000 with series prefixes NJ, NM, NP, NG, NH, NL, NK, NQ, NR, NS, NE, NN, NX, and NF found with the references G-7107, 7117, 7127, 7105, 7106, 7116, 7113, 7128, 7163, 7173, 7103, 7123, 7153, and 7143. By then, both the final modifications and the various components of military standardization had been applied.

Chassis Number

The administrative interpretation of the truck and more particularly of its chassis number begins with its location on the vehicle: depending on its model and/or its place of production, the number could be situated on the vertical side of the right longeron, near the front wheel or on the top side of that same longeron, but behind the cabin. It was made of four sequences, all of them explained below.

September 18, 1941, on the General Motors' test track at Milford, Michigan, a Chevrolet cargo shows off its potential to an attentive audience. The vehicle is on a 60% incline ramp. (General Motors A16389)

Above: April 20, 1941 at the Janesville Plant (code 21), Wisconsin. A common scene for U.S. Army suppliers, these YP-G 4112-YJ winchless cargo trucks are awaiting transfer. Don't put too much faith in the registration markings on the hoods, which indicate cargo trucks with winch. (Private collection)

Below: Fort Benning, February 5, 1941. Another example of the unreliable nature of Chevrolet's registration numbers with this winchless cargo dump truck YP-G 4112-YH: the registration indicates a winchless cargo truck. (Photo ATL-592025)

VEHICLE TYPE ACCORDING TO THE MASTER BOOK		
Series prefix & G-model	**Suffix**	**Body Type**
Classification for the 11,180 vehicles of the first series		
YP G-4112	YA	Telephone maintenance with winch
YP G-4112	YB	Winchless telephone maintenance
YP G-4112	YC	Telephone maintenance with winch and earth borer
YP G-4112	YG	Panel delivery
YP G-4112	YH	Winchless dump
YP G-4112	YJ	Winchless cargo
YP G-4112	YK	Tractor
YP G-4112	YL	Dump with winch
YP G-4112	YM	Cargo with winch
YP G-4112	YZ	Airfield service
YQ G-4103	YN	Cab over engine stake & platform (C.O.E. S&P)
YQ G-4112	YQ	Winchless long cargo
Classification for the 8,927 vehicles of the second series		
ZP G-4113	ZE	Cab only
ZP G-4105	ZG	Panel delivery
ZP G-4152	ZH	Winchless dump
ZP G-4165	ZK	Tractor
ZP G-4162	ZM	Dump with winch
ZP G-4163	ZL	Cargo with winch
ZP G-4174	ZQ	Winchless long cargo
Classification for the 135,230 vehicles of the third series		
NE G-7103	NF	Cab only
NG G-7105	NE	Field lighting
NF G-7143	NG	Panel delivery
NH G-7106	NH	Winchless dump
NJ G-7107	NJ	Winchless cargo
NK G-7113	NK	Tractor
NL G-7116	NL	Dump with winch
NM G-7117	NM	Cargo with winch
NN G-7123	NN	Cab over engine stake & platform
NP G-7127	NP	Winchless long cargo
NQ G-7128	NQ	Bomb service
NR G-7163	NR	Telephone maintenance with winch and earth borer
NS G-7173	NS	Telephone maintenance with winch
NX G-7153	NX	C.O.E. fire truck
NZ G-7133	NZ	Airfield crash
G-7129		Lowboy

CODE FOR THE YEAR AND MONTH OF PRODUCTION IN THE CHASSIS NUMBER												
	Jan	**Feb**	**Mar**	**Apr**	**May**	**Jun**	**Jul**	**Aug**	**Sep**	**Oct**	**Nov**	**Dec**
1941								8	9	10	11	12
1942	1	2	3	4	5	6	7	20	21	22	23	24
1943	13	14	15	16	17	18	19	32	33	34	35	36
1944	25	26	27	28	29	30	31	44	45	46	47	48
1945	37	38	39	40	41	42	43	56	57	58	59	60
1946	49	50	51	52	53	54	55					

Let us take the example of chassis number 8NM48-13034; this is how to interpret the vehicle:

"8": The first number indicates the assembly factory of the vehicle. (1: Flint, Michigan; 2: Tarrytown, New York; 3: Saint Louis, Missouri; 5: Kansas City, Kansas; 6: Oakland, California; 8: Atlanta, Georgia; 9: Norwood, Georgia; 14: Baltimore, Maryland; 20: Los Angeles, California; 21: Janesville, Wisconsin.) Our example was therefore built in the Chevrolet factory at Atlanta, Georgia.

"MN": These two letters indicate the Master Book Symbol, which established the type of vehicle (see table page 9, left-hand column); these must not be confused with the prefix of the serial number (center column). Whilst in the case of the G-7000 Chevrolet series the two symbols were identical, in the G-4000 series they were different. The two are therefore necessary to decipher the whole thing. Series numbers with prefixes YP, YQ, ZP, and ZQ of the first series only serve to determine the short or long wheelbase, whilst the Master Book symbols define the truck itself. Our example is an NM, which identifies it as a cargo truck with winch of the third series, in category NM G-7117 NM. If it had been from the first series, it would have been a YP G-4112 YM, and a ZP G-4163 ZM if from the second series.

"48": A one- or two-digit number, the third element represents the month and year of manufacture according to the manufacturer's own table (see table page 9). Our example, code 48, was therefore built in December 1944.

"13034": A four-digit minimum number in a digital sequence starting with 14001, indicates the assembly number of the vehicle. There is, however, no logical link between the Chevrolets' fourth element, because quantification counters were reset at 1001 each August 1, for a period of a year, and each assembly site had its own number series.

Our example is therefore the 13,034th 1½-ton Chevrolet, and it came out of its Atlanta factory during the period of August 1, 1944 to July 31, 1945, more precisely in December 1944.

This was the theory. In practice, there were a few flaws in the U.S. Army's administration. The Army's suppliers had to match specific chassis series numbers with a specific series of registrations, but

July 24, 1941. A convoy of brand-new Chevrolet trucks at Emeryville's Motor Supply Depot, California, arriving from the Los Angeles Plant (code 20) located a few miles away. (Photo U.S. Army SC-121783)

Above: The officer in charge of accepting this lot of cargo trucks G-7107-NJ will have no problem matching the trucks in his inventory as the registration numbers comply with U.S. Army norms. (U.S. Army Signal Corps)

Above, left: An example of a chassis number plate. Manufactured in the Norwood factory (9), this tractor truck (NK) dates from November 1943 (35) and was the 7,025th vehicle built at the factory since August 1, 1943. (Photo Th. Mahot)

the diversity of the Chevrolet production locations caused mistakes and mix-ups. For example, series of numbers due for cargo trucks were allocated to dump trucks and vice-versa. This certainly explains the lack of clarity of various technical manuals, which made no mention of hood numbers, only of type Gs, which were an integral part of the chassis number. It is therefore very important to take great care whilst examining photographs to identify a vehicle by its registration number.

2 The Series

YP-G-4112-YJ cargo truck displaying its characteristic slanted front hooks, its high bumper and its peculiar exhaust. (U.S. Army Signal Corps)

First Series, G-4112

Like General Motors, which allocated the type CCKWX to its famous 2½-ton truck, Chevrolet created the G-4112 type for its 1½-ton, 4x4s at the beginning of production.

Built between November 1940 and April 1941, these trucks were categorized as YP-G-4112 for a short chassis with a 145-inch wheelbase, and as YQ-G-4112 for a long chassis with a 175-inch wheelbase.

This YP-G-4112-YJ cargo truck's registration number is W-329859. The battery is located under the cabin and the fuel filter in the engine compartment. (U.S. Army Signal Corps)

As of April 1940, the prototype with winch made its debut at the Holabird Quartermaster Depot in Baltimore; it was followed by pre-series vehicles, and a swift production launch. The U.S. Army wanted its favorite 1½-ton range rejuvenated and taking precedence over the 2½-ton, the role of which was not yet clearly defined.

The Quartermaster Corps had a strong preference for this category, as it was widespread in the civilian range of car manufacturers. It is interesting to note that the creation and allocation of the G-4112 winchless dump truck was dictated by the need to dispose of the waste from cavalry units' horses, which were still common at that time.

To differentiate between the various versions produced in both wheelbase classes, Chevrolet added a two-letter suffix to the basic nomenclature (see table page 9). Thus, a YP-G-4112-YJ was a winchless cargo truck, 6,403 units built. The YP-G-4112-YM was a cargo truck with winch, 2,110 units built. YQ-G-4112-YQs were winchless long cargos (219 units), YGs were panel delivery trucks (54 units), YHs were winchless dump trucks (1,558 units), YLs were dump trucks with winch (284 units), YKs were tractors (8 units), YAs were telephone pole setters (115 units), YBs were telephone maintenance trucks (67 units), and YCs were telephone earth borers (81 units). Another 217 fire trucks Class 110 with no further classification were built. That made a total of 11,212 vehicles for this first series, which was split into four different contracts.

Shape

The chassis was traditional and made of two main longerons and crossbars supporting the three main parts of the vehicle, the engine block and the gearbox for the mechanical part, the cabin behind the whole engine/foredeck which could be disengaged, and a technical part at the rear above the drive axle with twin wheels.

When the vehicle was equipped with a winch, it could be found at the front, connected to a power takeoff (P.T.O.) via a cardan shaft with cross-brace located on the left of the gearbox. On the G-4112, with or without winch, the bumper was identical and the cable guide reel below it. On the telephone maintenance trucks, the rear winch was placed on a frame affixed to the chassis

Above: A YP-G-4112-YH cargo dump truck. This is a perfect illustration of its dual functionality, as a dump truck and a transport vehicle with the canvas and arches in place. (U.S. Army Signal Corps)

Below: Taken from technical manual TM 10-1202 is a view of the first series vehicle's cabin and dashboard. The instrumentation was replicated from civilian lines.

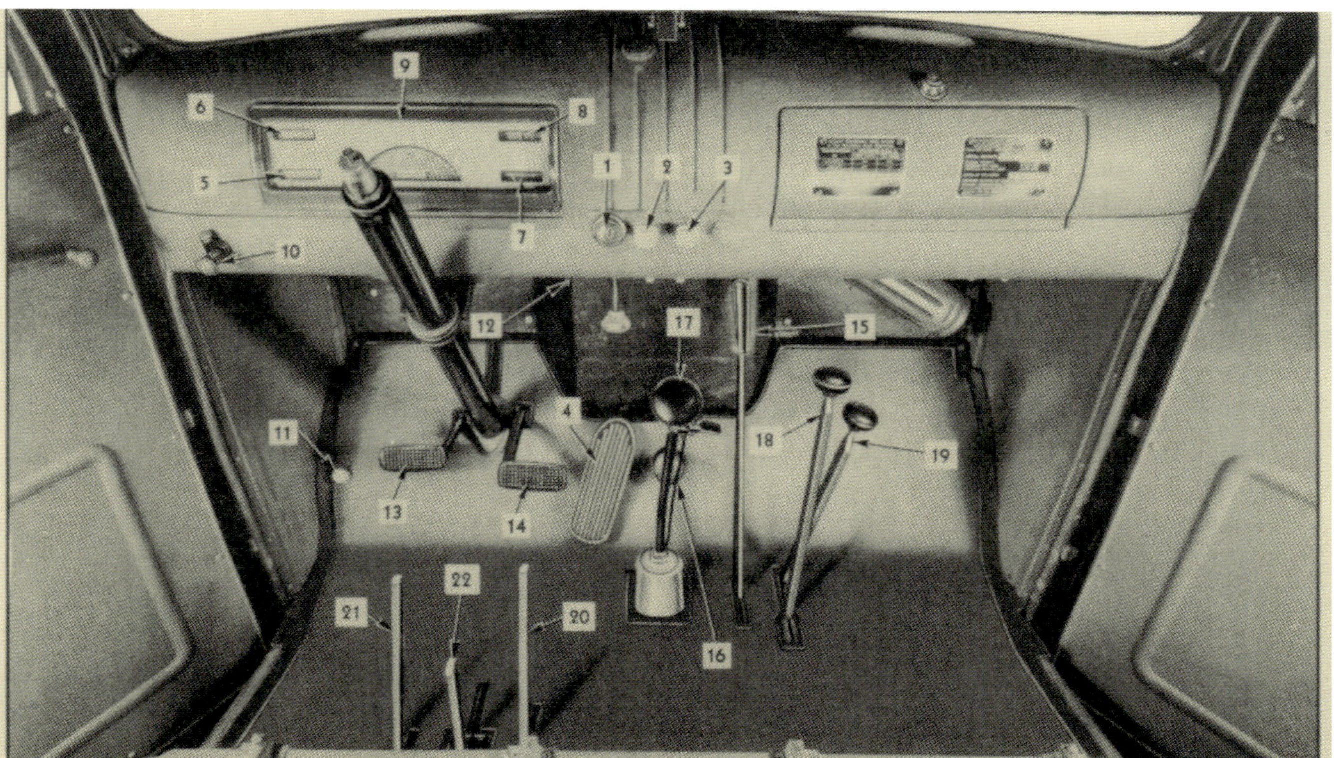

Fig. 1—Interior of cab, showing controls and instruments.

1—Ignition Switch
2—Hand Throttle
3—Carburetor Choke
4—Accelerator
5—Fuel Gauge
6—Temperature Indicator
7—Oil Gauge
8—Ammeter
9—Speedometer
10—Lighting Switch
11—Headlight Dimmer Switch
12—Instrument Light Switch
13—Clutch Pedal
14—Brake Pedal
15—Hand Brake Lever
16—Starter Switch Pedal
17—Transmission Gearshift Lever
18—Transfer Case Shifting Lever
19—Front Axle Control Lever
20—Hoist Valve Control Lever
21—Hoist Power Take-Off Lever
22—Winch Control Lever

and moved thanks to a single P.T.O.—or a double one when dealing with the auger version.

Mechanical

The Chevrolet G-4112 was fitted with a first-rate Model 216 engine, also referred to as BVA-1001, with six in-line cylinders, water-cooled, 3,860 cm^3, 93 hp 3,100 rpm. It was also connected via a single-disc clutch system to a General Motors-built four-speed and reverse gearbox, to a reductive transfer box, and to Banjo-type axles, also coming from General Motors. The electrics functioned with six volts from a battery located under the cabin floor. Most of the electrical components were from Delco-Remy. The braking system was a traditional hydraulic type with a single master cylinder and a four-wheel slave cylinder. The handbrake had a direct action on the rear axle.

The fuel tank, with a capacity of 30 gallons, was positioned between the longerons, right behind or vertically behind the cabin depending on the model of the rear bodywork. Tires were 7.5x20 8 ply. The theoretical average cruising range was 270 miles, with an average consumption of 4.3 miles per gallon (54.7 liters per 100 kilometers).

Design

The outline of the Chevrolet G-4112 was made up of various elements that evolved over the years, adapting to the needs of its users and the need for standardization. Here are some of the more common elements:

A typical layout for a Chevy G-4112 chassis. The battery can be seen under the cabin's position, as yet unmoved to the side of the right longeron, and the fuel filter is located in the engine compartment.

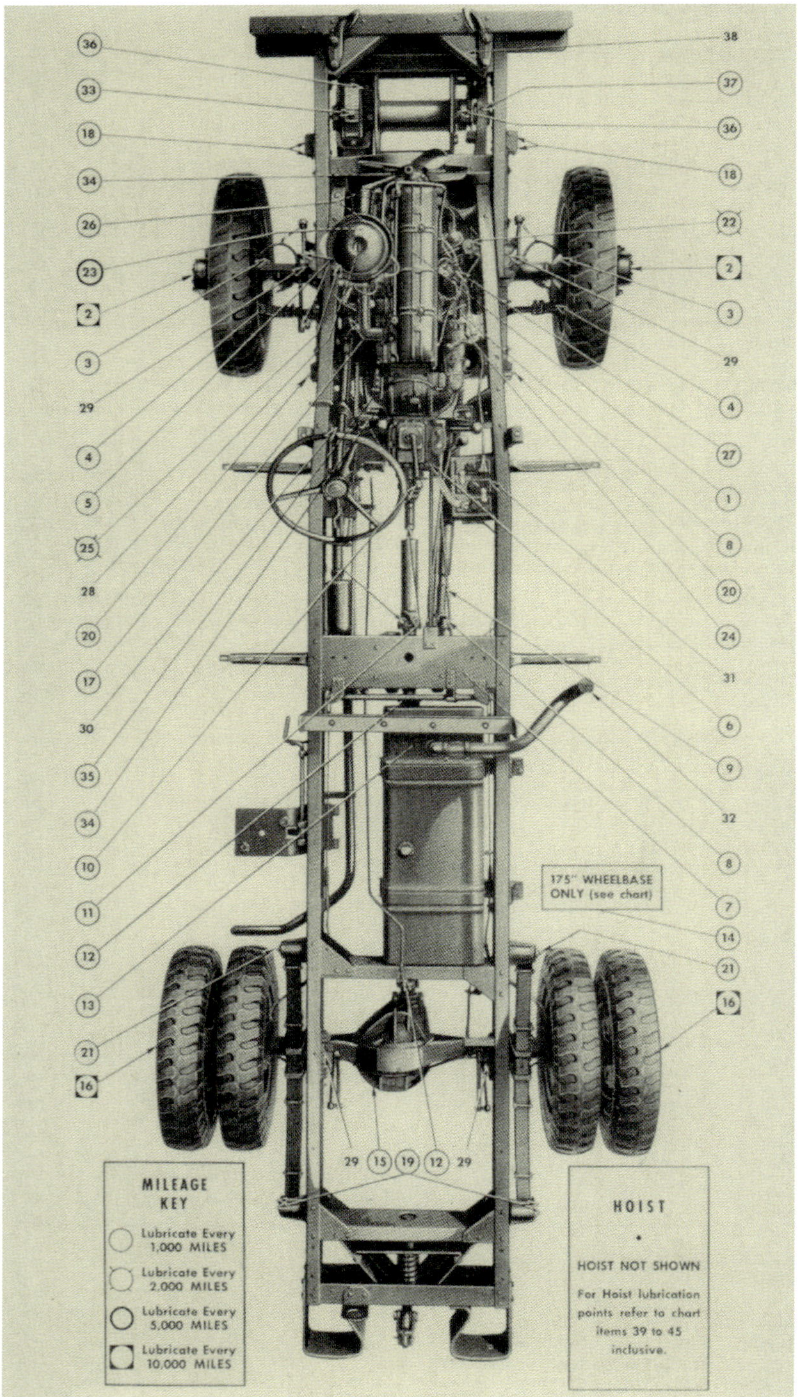

Right: The Oakland factory (code 6), California. A G-4112 cabin is being assembled on a chassis that has already been fitted with all the mechanical elements. The number of levers suggests that this will be a winchless cargo truck. (Private collection)

Below: Flint Factory (code 1), Michigan. Russell K. Miller is fine-tuning the rocker arm and valves on the engine, before sending the motor to the assembly line. (General Motors)

- The radiator's protective grille was made of two folded rods, each securing half the coiled rods, and a central vertical one.
- The bumper was at the same height whether equipped with a winch or not, though minus the cable guide roller.
- The absence of blackout light on the right wing.
- Small blue lens marker lights.
- Tow hooks at the front, strongly slanted towards the inside of the chassis.
- The stamped Chevrolet logo on the sides of the engine compartment, although it would only appear towards the end of the G-4115 production run, around April 1941.
- The last portion of the exhaust line, coming out in front of the rear right mudguard, at the same level as the Banjo axle hub.

The cabin originated from civilian production with its all-in-one-piece instruments that—apart from the odometer which had a rotary hand—made use of linear reading (water temperature, oil pressure, amperage, fuel gauge); an uncommon luxury for an army truck, the seats were upholstered.

One of the particularities of the G-4112's range was that it had three different machines for the Signal Corps telephone missions, contrary to the G-7000 series, which had only allocated two types of trucks for the same purpose. There was the YP-G-4112-YA telephone pole setter (referred to as K-43 in transmissions), with a winch at the back to use with a lifting device; the YP-G-4112-YB telephone maintenance or K-42 which had no winch; and the YP-G-4112-YC telephone earth borer, equipped with an auger controlled by a P.T.O. as well as a rear winch, named K-44-A or K-44-B depending on what drilling equipment it was fitted with.

Second Series, G-4000 Assimilated

These Chevrolets were the link between the G-4112s and the assimilated Chevrolet such as the G-7000s of standard production. They were the first step towards

Above: October 1943. An exercise in installing phone lines with the RL-26 reel. The shape of the Chevrolet 1½-ton, 4x4 cargo body is very specific: with its protective angle iron, it cannot be confused with any other vehicle. (U.S. Army C-3608)

Left: The right rear of the cabin defines the production series. There is no recess either at the foot of the cabin, nor in the running board as the battery is located below the floor. This is therefore a vehicle from the G-4112 series. (Signal Corps)

the final evolution of this type of truck. Built between April and September 1941, they were referred to as ZP-G-4000 for the 145-inch wheelbase chassis and ZQ-G-4000 for the 175-inch wheelbase chassis. Just like the Willys Slat Grill or General Motors CCKW in 1941, this intermediary series made the first structural changes. It was the smallest series of the three, which comprised:

- ZP-G-4163-ZM, cargo truck with winch, 6,770 units built.
- ZP-G-4174-ZQ, winchless long cargo, 35 units built.
- ZP-G-4105-ZG, panel delivery truck, 146 units built.
- ZP-G-4152-ZH, winchless dump truck, 1,384 units built.

The radiator grille is similar to the first series with its central vertical bar and its two coiled side bars, but the bumper hooks are straighter. (U.S. Army Signal Corps)

The battery is now visible outside the right longeron, the running board has been recut and the cabin has a recess. With the same configuration, this ZP-G-4162-ZL cargo dump truck is typical of the second series. (U.S. Army Signal Corps)

- ZP-G-4162-ZL, dump truck with winch, 500 units built.
- ZP-G-4165-ZK, tractor, 89 units built.

All 8,924 of these units were taken in the same contract.

Shape

The overall shape of these second-generation vehicles was similar to the first series, with, however, two main changes: the battery was moved from the bottom of the cabin to be placed on the outside of the right longeron, which required shortening the footboard and creating a recess in the lower cabin. Very early on in production, the bumper became smaller for the winchless version. On the winch version, the bumper retained the same height but was placed lower, which afforded the cable guide reel better protection thanks to the recess it created.

Only three ZP-G4113-ZE chassis cabs were included in the second series, one registered as W-80920. Adapted by Heil, it became the only Chevrolet 1½-ton, 4x4 lubricant truck. (U.S. Army Signal Corps)

Mechanical

Overall, the mechanical elements remained similar to the G-4112 configuration, including the fuel filter, which was still located on the right side of the engine compartment. The only significant modification was the relocation of the handbrake mechanism, to the transfer box. Note one important change in the main braking system: whilst keeping the master cylinder, a Bendix hydrovac was added and the canalizations modified. The electrical circuit remained positively grounded.

Design

The main constituents of this series of seven vehicles remained unchanged, although the sides of the engine compartment now bore the Chevrolet brand stamp and the upholstery of the seats was replaced by faux leather. During the course of production, the blue

Above: View of the G-4000 assimilated cabin. After this series, it would be completely militarized. The dual-function windshield wipers, for instance, would be replaced with standard military equipment. (TM 10-1431)

Right: May 18, 1942 at a Northern Ireland port, a Chevy is being unloaded, displaying the top of the vehicle and its general structure, especially the pronounced sides of the body. (AP Wirephoto)

marker lights were replaced by blackout fender lights. The last part of the exhaust line was modified to go behind the mudguard and emerge closer to the main body, thus helping in crossing deep fords. The tow hooks on the bumper were straightened up and were now held by three fixation points rather than two.

The dump truck axles came solely from Hercules Steel Products, whilst in the next series of type G-7000, three suppliers were chosen: Hercules, Hell, and Perfection. Gar Wood Industries was the sole supplier of the front winches and P.T.O.s for all versions.

During maneuvers in October 1941, North Carolina, this second-series Chevrolet cargo with winch, registration number W-335359, is seen here carrying out its primary function: supplying cavalry units with fodder. (U.S. Army SC-124085)

August 1941, outside the factory at Atlanta, Georgia (code 8). These G.I.s have just taken possession of a lot of ZP-G-4163-ZM cargo trucks with winch, to transport them to Camp Stewart, in the same state. The trucks still display factory signage, which will be removed on arrival. Only the registration number and the vehicle's configuration allow us to identify with certainty the vehicle type, W-342004, being the front vehicle. (U.S. Army SC-122060)

Considering that Chevrolet and General Motors were from the same commercial family, it might be surprising to see that the cabins were so different. Whilst they looked similar on the outside, they evolved from two different matrices, the positioning of some of the dashboard instrumentation, like the headlamp or brake controls, being different

The location of the side mirror on the top hinge of the driver's door remained unchanged throughout the Chevrolet line's production, but it was modified on the CCKW. In the same way, the overall structure of the cabin, which was all metal on the Chevrolet production line (apart from the bomb carrier), moved towards the canvas roof of the General Motors line.

October 1942, at HQ 1st Service Command, Boston, Massachusetts. One of the particularities of the G-4000 assimilated was the new exhaust line, now attached higher up and behind the mudguard. (U.S. Army SC-144442)

June 25, 1944 in Puerto Rico, Military Police conduct a routine inspection of a driver's mission order. The configuration of the truck and its registration, W-332578, make it a second-series cargo truck with winch, ZP-G 4163-ZM. (Wide World Photo A-42157)

Registration number W-351009 applies to this G-7107-NJ. The radiator grille is of the coiled type. The vehicle does not as yet carry the blackout drive. (U.S. Army Signal Corps)

The transformation of the vehicle is coming to an end. Easily recognizable thanks to the location of the battery on the right longeron, the G-7000 assimilated also had its fuel filter there; this setup required a recess in the upper part of the running board. (U.S. Army SC-144436)

Third Series, G-7000 Assimilated

The G-7000 assimilated was the end result of the 1½-ton, 4x4 Chevy's evolution, a little like the Jeep MB for Willys, the GPW for Ford or the CCKW for General Motors. But despite its apparent finality, the vehicles continued evolving and a number of modifications took place throughout their production. Whilst the machines of the first and second series were mostly used by the U.S. Army, a large majority of the G-7000s were sent to allied nations.

Shape

There were no major transformations, apart from the fuel filter relocating from the engine compartment to the outside of the right longeron, just in front of the battery. This necessitated a modification of the course of the pipes and the creation of a recess in the right-side running board.

When the blackout drive was introduced, Chevrolet used a special kit to update the vehicles that were not equipped with the new headlamp. It was mostly made up of a metal sheet that was positioned over the grille, protecting the right headlamp. (U.S. Army Signal Corps)

A typical grille from the end of the production run. It is simply made of vertical rods, while a lateral protrusion protects the blackout light. (U.S. Army)

The side recesses for the battery and the fuel filter can be found on all models in the series, as with this panel delivery truck G-7105-NG. (U.S. Army SC-132247)

Quickly, the radiator grille was simplified, the series of coiled bars being replaced with 13 vertical rods. After the blackout drive was installed, a support was fitted above the left light's guard. This adaption necessitated a modification kit for the vehicles already delivered to the Army. Later on, the grilles were produced with an appendage on the side and the light located on the wing.

But it was on the inside where the biggest modifications occurred: the dashboard panel that comprised the dials, gauges, and controls was replaced by five independent military dials and the seats were covered in strong khaki canvas. Smaller details could also be noticed, like the modification of the hood's hinges to match the design of those used on the CCKW. It should also be noted that the Chevrolet stamp on the engine compartment was removed, as the Army wished to maintain neutrality with its suppliers.

Mechanical

At the beginning of production, the Chevrolet Model 216/BVA-1001 was still the engine used, before being replaced by Model 235/BVA-1001. There was no major difference between them except for the lubrication system and the intake and exhaust manifolds.

They were both water-cooled six-cylinder, 235.5 in^3, 93 hp, 3,100 rpm, and were linked through a dry-running single-disc clutch of 10¾ in. to a four-speed and reverse gearbox and a two-gear transfer box, allowing the activation of the all-wheel drive. Note the inversion of the electrical circuit's polarity: it was now negatively grounded.

If a winch was installed at the front of the vehicle, it was always the 2U512 model from Gar Wood

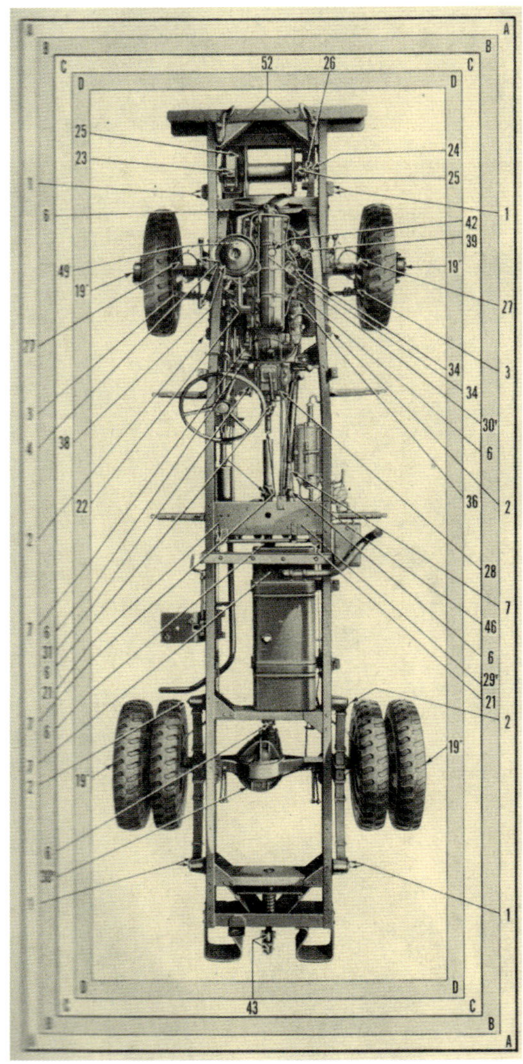

This extract from the lubrication chart in TM 10-1557 shows the relocation of the battery and the fuel filter to the side of the right longeron. (Extract TM 10-1557)

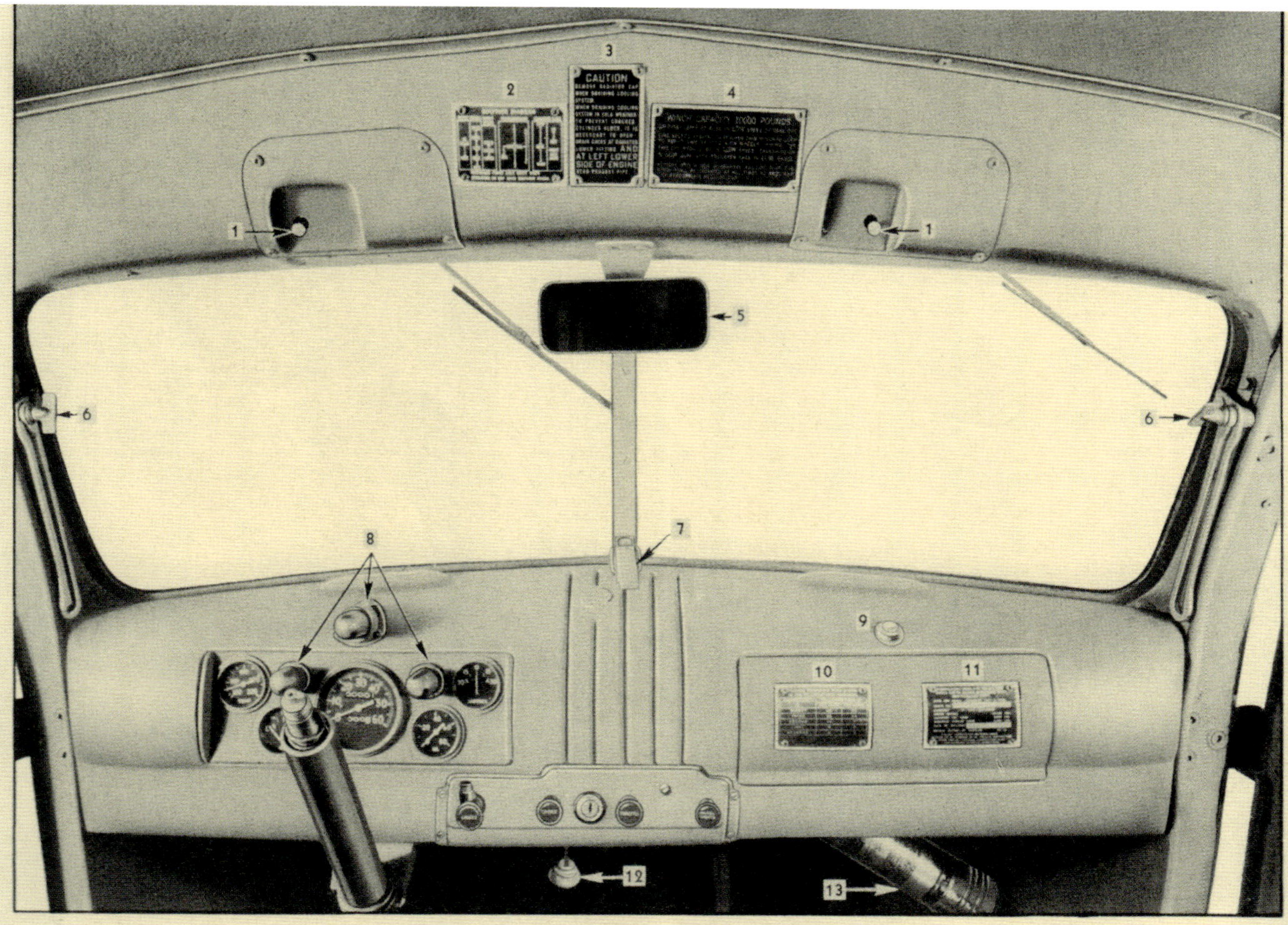

Fig. 2—Interior of Cab Instruction Plates, etc.

1—Windshield Wiper Switch
2—Shifting Diagram Plate
3—Cooling System Draining Caution Plate
4—Winch Operation Instruction Plate
5—Rear View Mirror
6—Windshield Quadrant Adjusting Screws
7—Windshield Center Lock
8—Instrument Lights
9—Glove Compartment Lock
10—Maximum Permissible Road Speeds Plate
11—Serial Number and Load Data Plate
12—Cowl Ventilator Control Lever
13—Fire Extinguisher

Above: The design of the cabin in its almost final state; only a few elements will change, like the ignition switch which is still there, not as yet replaced by the standard manual model. (Extract TM 10-1127)

Right: A photo taken by the Signal Corps, on July 2, 1942, at Fort Sam Houston, Texas, displaying the contents of the Chevrolet 1½-ton, 4x4 toolkit. (U.S. Army SC-146516)

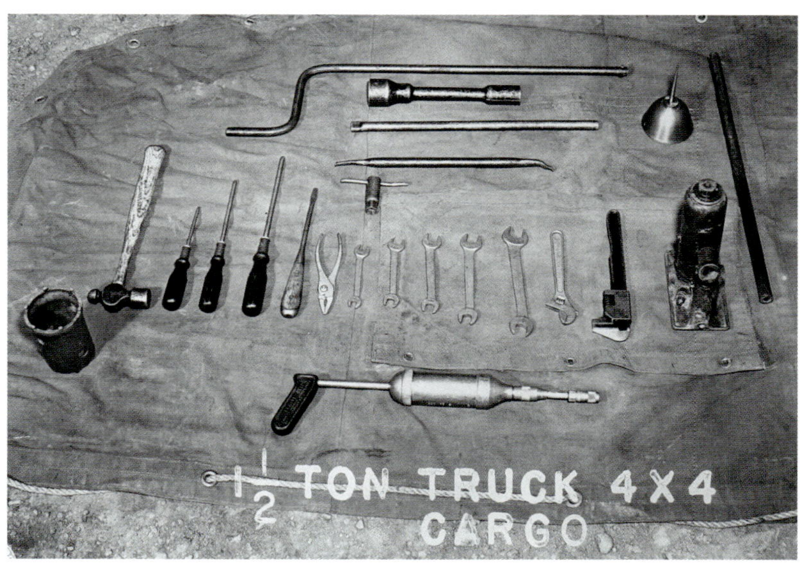

Industries, with a 10,000-lb. capacity. However, to facilitate the supply, Hell Company also supplied winches under the reference JJ-104-B. They were of the interlocking type and always controlled from a power takeoff—single or double depending on the type of the vehicle—either from Gar Wood Industries or the Spicer Manufacturing Company. These winches had two cable winding-up speeds and one for unwinding. It was also possible to unwind manually by deactivating the interlocking system.

Purpose

In the final analysis the Chevrolet 1½-ton, 4x4 was not that popular with the Army. Their creation seemed to stem from a mistake and/or a need to please a specific element of the armed forces. Compared to Dodge, Jeep, or General Motors, their numbers were not significant, though the diversity of the models could serve many purposes. Considering the models with and without winches, for example, this assimilated series G-7000 boasted no fewer than 15 different models.

There were two reasons for the lack of interest. The first was that driving it required a certain amount of finesse, especially when the engine was cold: due to its lubrication system the engine needed to warm up slowly, which was not always practical. The second reason was due to the size and category of the whole family. Whilst the Chevy was adapted to its missions when first created, the evolution of the war meant that this was no longer the case. Even if at the time the lowboys pried open a window of opportunity, it was quickly shut again, and it could not compete with the size and bulk of the Dodge WC ¾-ton. It was too small to compare with the new 2½-ton, 6x6s whether from General Motors, International Harvester, or Studebaker.

But in the end, was the 1½-ton, 4x4 Chevrolet not a pawn in an internal business power struggle? It can't have made that much of a difference for General Motors, G-7000 or CCKW: they were filling order forms. Apart from the very specific ones like the telephone maintenance, turret trainer, field lighting or fire trucks, which were not replaced, other trucks saw

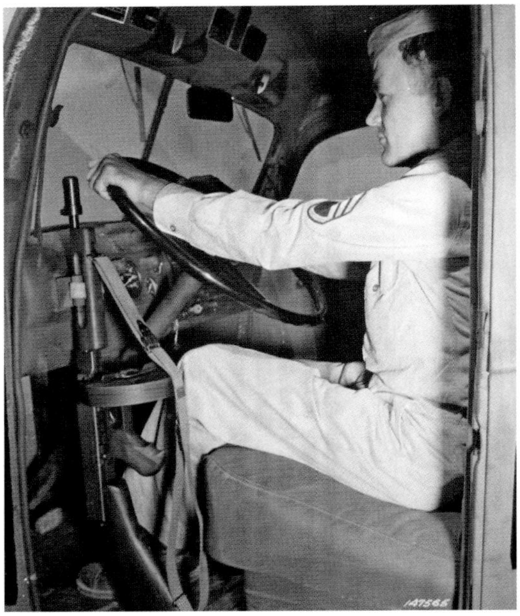

Right: A variety of tests were conducted to find the best way to fit personal weapons inside the cabin. S/Sgt John Ontocheck's Thompson submachine gun is installed here inside a G-7000 assimilated Chevy. (U.S. Army SC-147565)

Below: September 1942, Desert Training Center. Amongst a wide range of vehicles, the Chevrolet G-7107-NJ participated in a full-scale survey, designed to test military-type tires to assess their strength and resistance and therefore plan future needs, both for supplies and replacements, in order to prevent accidents. (U.S. Army Signal Corps)

their missions easily fulfilled by the 2½-ton, 6x6 line, which became the absolute norm. But what were they supposed to do with the orders already in place, most of them dating from 1942?

The few orders from the end of 1943 and 1944 were delivered only to update the existing fleet of small units, and to fulfill the limited needs for trucks of that size. As for the rest, the Army only kept a small proportion of them. Of a total of 138,166 G-7000 assimilated, with standard cabin—take away specific orders from the Defense Aid program, which can be recognized by the structure of the order number, that is 10,193 vehicles making up 7.6 percent of the production run; and also take away the 67,613 vehicles for Lend-Lease, representing 50.2 percent of the deliveries—only 60,360 Chevrolet 1½-ton, 4x4s were utilized by the U.S. Army, some 43.31 percent of the production run.

Right: Test results were surprising: after an average of 1,550 miles driven on various types of terrain (sand, earth and stone) the tire casings tore. (U.S. Army Signal Corps)

Below: Partial view of Camp Blanding, Florida in September 1942. Chevy G-7177-NMs are counted in tens amongst Dodges, GMCs, Jeeps, and other military vehicles. (U.S. Army SC-147220)

3 Cargo Trucks

In this category, three models were ordered, making a total of 115,657 vehicles. But the U.S. Army received only 113,461, as 2,196 of them had their orders cancelled.

Right: At the Desert Training Center in Indio, California, June 8, 1942. Each vehicle was the subject of a photographic report, a kind of ID card for this YP-G-4112-YJ. (U.S. Army SC-141791)

Below: A typical example of an early production winchless cargo truck. This YP-G 4112-YJ was photographed at Fort Benning in October 1941, with Private F.K. Kurtz at the wheel. The marking on the door is that of the 161st Signal Photographic Company (S.P.C.), one of the most famous units to whom we owe many of the images from World War II. (U.S. Army SC-124029)

Cargo trucks with short (145-inch) or long (175-inch) wheelbases, with or without winches, represented around 70 percent of the 1½-ton, 4x4 Chevrolets. Within this number, winchless short-wheelbase cargos numbered 86,871 (6,403 G-4112s, and 80,468 G-7107s); short-wheelbase cargos with winch represented 26,206 units (2,110 G-4112s, 6,770 G-4163s, and 130 G-7127s); and long cargo trucks totaled 384 (219 G-4112s, 35 G-4174s, and 130 G-7127s). Delivery figures from the Defense Aid program and the Lend-Lease agreement indicated that 66,392 units of three different models were exported, of which 52 were winchless long cargo trucks; unfortunately, there is no detail concerning the short cargo trucks.

A Body for All Occasions

There were no specialized assignments for this type of vehicle; it could transport goods and men alike.

The creation of long-wheelbase vehicles came from the need to have a transport carriage big enough to take large and lengthy items without them sticking out of the back.

The technical part of the truck was composed of a metallic plate with three drop-sides and five or seven arches to hold the protection canvas. The two lateral drop-sides were made with a rotating part, which turned into a seat when the vehicle was used for troop transport. Built by the Edw. G. Budd Manufacturing

Above: Overseas units did not spare their Chevys, as it was faster and more flexible than the G.M.C. Seen here is a YP-G-4112-YJ whose tow hooks have been strangely inverted. (U.S. Army Air Forces 67281-A.C.)

Right: London, June 14, 1942. A rear view of a YP-G 4112-YJ with an early cargo body; note its recessed lights, and the reflectors located on the outside of the reinforcement panel. (ACME BC-651818)

Company, the external dimensions were 113 x 86½ inches and 193 x 96 inches for the short and long types respectively.

The cargo truck's body had a very peculiar design: the two sides at the back created a triangular reinforcement, which caused the presence of large horizontal side structures, most probably to improve the rigidity of the sides with the back panel. This concept only left a usable width of 70 inches for the short wheelbase (a width loss of 16½ inches) and 89½ inches for the long wheelbase (a width loss of 6½ inches only). The other important difference was the side panels, only 14 inches high on the short wheelbase and 42 inches high on the long wheelbase at the beginning of production.

Above: At the Chief of Ordnance Detroit office, a G-7117-NM with a wooden cargo body. The vehicle is exhibited among other vehicles ordered by the Ordnance Department. (ORD 2550)

Left: New Guinea, November 6, 1943. The South Pacific theater was a real ordeal for vehicles that often had to deal with impassable mud. This Chevrolet G-7107-NJ, registered 34767, belongs to the U.S. Navy. (Wide World Photos A-34828)

CENSUS OF REGISTRATIONS ALLOCATED TO WINCHLESS CARGO TRUCKS				
Contract	Year	Body Type	Registration	Total Units
W-398-QM-8278	1940	YP-G 4112-YJ winchless short cargo	(W-320560 to W-324604) (W-324605 to W-325073) (W-328951 to W-330839)	6,403
W-398-QM-10328	1941	G-7107-NJ winchless short cargo	(345641 to 347272) (347741 to 348740) (349739 to 350393) (350769 to 351488) (349361 to 349410) (348841 to 349360) (351769 to 352777) (356916 to 357465) (357651 to 358300) (358641 to 358940)	7,086
W-398-QM-10939	1942	G-7107-NJ winchless short cargo	(359275 to 360901)	1,627
W-398-QM-11510	1942	G-7107-NJ winchless short cargo	(371446 to 371745) (371746 to 389178) (390024 to 390268) (393514 to 393868) (394869 to 395621) (396002 to 398927) (3101874 to 3101883) (3218319 to 3218878) (3259288 to 3259337) (3284244 to 3293095)	31,484
W-374-ORD-6582	1942	G-7107-NJ winchless short cargo	(3399524 to 3410335 of which 500 without body)	10,812
DA-W-398-QM-8	1941	G-7107-NJ winchless short cargo	No registration number	24
DA-W-398-QM-252	1941	G-7107-NJ winchless short cargo	No registration number	6,704
W-374-ORD-018-517	1944	G-7107-NJ winchless short cargo	(3440079 to 3455166) (3473470 to 3473948) (3480357 to 3486274 of which 468 units without body) (3506501 to 3507046 of which 511 units without body)	23,096 units and 1,065 for the Corps of Engineers without registration numbers going to the U.S.M.C. and the Navy. This does not take into consideration the 1,362 vehicles with bare chassis that were converted to winchless cargo trucks.
Notes: The purchase orders totaled 87,236 vehicles of which 86,871 were received by the Ordnance Department. 1,479 units were supplied to the Army without the cargo body. According to the Ordnance Department Administrative and Tactical Vehicles Report of October 1, 1945, 479 registration numbers (3292616 to 3293095) were not used.				

Up until June 1943, these two cargo bodies remained mostly the same; after that, though, numerous small differences began appearing, the most obvious one being the rear light brackets. Early in production, these were distanced from the vehicle's rear to be hidden under the platform; later, for easier access, they were almost level with it, the brackets having been shortened.

Wooden Frames

During the first half of 1943, wooden frames for short-wheelbase trucks began appearing. These were manufactured by various carpentry workshops, including furniture and piano makers. The change meant a saving of more than 350 kg of steel per truck. These combined wooden elements with metallic pieces to strengthen the joints. The wide variety of manufacturers taking the orders meant that the various subcontracted work was not always identical, despite stringent specification requirements. This new frame was relatively easy to build and assemble, but the wood had limited strength. Whilst the bottom fared well with the various cargos, this wasn't the case with the drop-sides or the cantilevered seats, which were put under severe strain.

Above: Late 1941, during the First Army's large-scale maneuvers in North Carolina. These trucks, armed with D.C.A. machine guns, belong to the 209th Coast Artillery Regiment, battery E. (U.S. Army SC-133899)

Left: February 26, 1942, Punta Salinas, Puerto Rico. Maintenance of a cargo truck YP-G 4112-YJ belonging to the 123rd Anti-Aircraft Artillery Regiment. (U.S. Army SC-132552)

CENSUS OF REGISTRATIONS ALLOCATED TO CARGO TRUCKS WITH WINCH				
Contract	Year	Body Type	Registration	Total Units
W-398-QM-8278	1941	YP-G 4112-YM short cargo with winch	(W-325074 to W-326802) (W-330840 to W-330965) (W-326803 to W-327057)	2,110
W-398-QM-9402	1941	ZP-G 4163-ZM short cargo with winch	(W-332066 to W-335851) (W-339995 to W-342977) W-332064	6,770
W-398-QM-10328	1941	G-7117-NM short cargo with winch	353244 (347273 to 347422) (349411 to 349459) (350394 to 350513) (351489 to 351618) (352784 to 352933) (357466 to 357615) (358301 to 358550) (358941 to 359140) [1]	1,200
W-398-QM-10939	1942	G-7117-NM short cargo with winch	(360902 to 362126) [2]	1,225
W-398-QM-11510	1942	G-7117-NM short cargo with winch	(389179 to 390023) (390269 to 393513) 3257838 (393869 to 394868) (395622 to 396001) (3293096 to 3296275) (3410336 to 3412279)	10,596
DA-W-398-QM-8	1942	G-7117-NM short cargo with winch	No registration number	2,500
DA-W-398-QM-252	1942	G-7117-NM short cargo with winch	No registration number	900
W-374-ORD-018-517	1944	G-7117-NM short cargo with winch	(3437343 to 3440078) [3]	2,736

Notes:

1. Purchase order reduced by 541 units
2. Purchase order reduced by 1,012 units
3. Purchase order reduced by 278 units

The purchase orders totaled 28,037 vehicles, of which 26,206 were received by the Ordnance Department.

According to the Ordnance Department Administrative and Tactical Vehicles Report of October 1, 1945, registration numbers 3439803 to 3440078 were not used, a total of 276 registration numbers.

Composite Frame

In early 1944, the problem was solved by using a composite frame. It combined wooden flooring and longerons with steel sides. These new mixed bodies were easily recognizable by the bolt heads attaching the steel sides to the wooden frame.

A secondary development saw the replacement of the wooden transversal longerons with steel. From January 1945, due to the war winding down, restrictions on metals became less stringent and the manufacturers had to start thinking about the durability of the machines in the aftermath. Trucks with any wooden

Motor Pool, Fort Lewis, Washington State, August 1942. Chevrolet cargos stack up in the hundreds. All the vehicles are new and have not as yet been allocated to any units, but the canvas roofs are already suffering weather damage. (U.S. Army SC-142772)

August 1941, Private Louis Kreitzman is checking Sergeant William Jones's mission order. They are both part of the 163rd S.P.C. at Fort Sam Houston, Texas. (U.S. Army SC-148077)

components were discarded for all-steel ones, this particularly while the vehicle upgrades were in force.

Service-proof

The 1½-ton, 4x4 line was ultimately never going to be competitive, and although many units were satisfied with the ride, the infantry was not. Indeed, both Dodge VFs and Chevy G-4112 cargos were unsuitable for combat missions and their demands. They were either too small or too large: too small to effectively transport thousands of G.I.s from A to B, and too large and conspicuous for reconnaissance missions.

Left: Fort Sheridan, Illinois, October 1942. With or without winch, short or long chassis, from late 1940 until mid-1942, these trucks readily took on any task required of them, including, as seen here, unloading rubble via a ramp especially dug for the purpose. (U.S. Army SC-144812)

Below: Trials of the 1½-ton, 4x4 were undertaken for several months where drivers had to negotiate rugged training tracks. In between the ½- or ¾-, and the 2½-ton, the Chevrolet was a highly adaptable vehicle, whose engine torque worked wonders where others failed because of their lack of a mechanical gearbox and their bulky size. (U.S. Army Signal Corps)

Above: Fort Monmouth, New Jersey, 1941. A line of Signal Corps Chevrolet YP-G-4112-YJs. All members of the transmission services and specialists from other corps went through this training school. (U.S. Army SC-120534)

Below: The magnitude of the work and the size of the transmission units meant that the 1½-ton, 4x4 was the ideal size. In the early 1940s the Signal Corps fleet also included K-51 and K-70 vans as well as telephone maintenance K-43s and earth borer K-44s. (U.S. Army SC-120535)

CENSUS OF REGISTRATIONS ALLOCATED TO LONG-WHEELBASE CARGO TRUCKS				
Contract	**Year**	**Body Type**	**Registration**	**Total Units**
W-398-QM-8278	1941	YQ-G 4112-YQ	(W-328310 to W-328400) (W-331556 to W-331683)	219
W-398-QM-9402	1941	ZP-G 4174-ZQ	(W-335852 to W-335886)	35 units, all with a front winch
W-398-QM-10328	1941	G-7127-NP	(347423 to 347442) (348741 to 348760) (352934 to 352973)	80
DA-W-398-QM-8	1942	G-7127-NP	No registration number	50

Left: The long wheelbase Chevrolet is easily recognizable by its cantilevered rear. Fresh from the assembly lines, this YQ-G 4112-YQ poses for Army catalogs. (U.S. Army ORD-270-1-41)

Below: Built on the base of a winchless YQ-G 4112-YQ long cargo, this 16-seater bus from the Air Force Air Transport Command was mostly made with wooden panels and other bits cannibalized from various Chevys, as shown by the hood, which belongs to a short cargo. (U.S. Army Signal Corps)

The Chevrolet firm regularly exhibited its vehicles during patriotic parades. This long ZP-G 4174-ZQ was customized to showcase a number of the subcomponents that Chevrolet manufactured. On display here are aluminum aviation parts and components of its famous Banjo axle. (General Motors)

However, as early as the end of 1940, the Corps of Engineers and the Signal Corps, amongst others, found these 4x4 trucks perfectly suited to their needs.

It is important to note that when this line was created, the U.S. Army did not as yet have units that used heavy materials, and the 1½-ton, 4x4s, together with a few 4-ton, 6x6s, met the specific needs of a peacetime army. But despite being regularly replaced with 2½-ton, 6x6s, the units that did use the 1½-ton, 4x4s, would take them all the way to Germany.

In 1945, a massive upgrade program of the fleet was put in place. In the case of the Chevrolet 1½-ton, 4x4, 532 winchless cargo trucks and 942 with winch were refurbished. Six firms would share the work: Bellingham Iron Works, Thomas Bryan Co., Coleman Motor, Espy Paving & Construction, Florida Aircraft, and Southern Iron & Equipment.

4 Panel Delivery Trucks

Closed steel-bodied Chevrolets were referred to as panel delivery trucks in the U.S. Army. All came out of the factory with the same specifications, and it was only after they had been delivered that the Signal Corps customized some of them as radio trucks.

There were 4,034 of them, 145-inch short-wheelbase trucks, representing 2.26 percent of the 1½-ton, 4x4 Chevrolet production. This number was split into 54 G-4112s, 146 G-4105s, and 3,834 G-7105s. The delivery figures of the Defense Aid program amounted to 475 vehicles, whilst those of the Lend-Lease agreement 180, all exported to Great Britain.

Vans

Directly derived from civilian production, the panel body, notwithstanding some modifications, was

Right: As a service vehicle, the panel truck had a very basic interior, with no partition between the front and rear; the sides were simple panels with no insulation. (U.S. Army HQD 269-2-41)

Below: February 13, 1945, Holabird Signal Depot at Baltimore, Maryland. The war is nearly over in Europe and is proceeding apace in the Pacific. In the United States, depots are bursting with matériel ready for transportation to the various theaters. Seen here are mostly Chevrolet panel delivery trucks. At that time stock levels were around 8,000 vehicles, all intended for the Signal Corps. (U.S. Army P-13-2-45-711)

Above: Reykjavik, Iceland, March 7, 1942. This panel delivery YP-G 4112-YG is being unloaded from the USAT *McCauley*. (U.S. Army SC-131837-R)

that which had equipped various Chevrolet army ambulances since 1930. These vans were first used as transport or service vehicles before some were converted to radio trucks.

In its full steel version, the Chevrolet panel was used as a transport vehicle, photo lab, a chaplain's vestry in the armored and infantry divisions, and as supply vehicle for the Clubmobiles of the American Red Cross, as well as any other mission requiring an enclosed vehicle for the transport of fragile goods.

Radio Vehicles

In its elementary form, the U.S. Army Chevrolet panel delivery dates back to 1940, but it was only in early 1942 that it would be converted into a radio vehicle. Up until then, long-distance radio communications with mobile posts were mostly conducted with SCR-197s installed in the GMC AF-361 type K-18 truck, with its K-19 trailer. In early spring 1942, the new SCR-299 radio transceiver, smaller and more powerful, was conceived. The conception of the K-51 required three players: Chevrolet for the vehicle, the Signal Corps for the specification and Hallicrafters Co. Inc. for the equipment and installation of the radio equipment.

Left: This panel G-7105-NG, registration number 3103517, is stuck in the mud of Guadalcanal. As shown by the markings on the hood, it belongs to the 6th Combat Camera Unit of the Thirteenth U.S. Army Air Force. (U.S. Army Air Forces A-44046)

A storage trunk was affixed to each external side; also added were a mounting base for the antenna and a large reel of phone cable. The roof supported the main antenna and a hole was fashioned for a ventilator. Between the driving seat and the main body, a partition with headrests for the crew was fitted. Whilst the panel delivery included three different types, only the third version, the G-7105-NG, corresponded to the radio frame. Once transformed in this manner, the vehicles were sent to Hallicrafters Co. Inc. to receive their transmission equipment.

Comprising a BC-610 transmitter, BC-312 and BC-342 receptors, a BC-614 amplifier, a BC-729 regulator, and a BC-211 frequency meter, the SCR-299 usually worked on a frequency scale of 2 to 8 Mhz, that could be stretched from 1 to 18 Mhz with conversion kits, its theoretical action radius being 100 miles—though during favorable conditions in the Pacific, some communications achieved 2,300 miles. Its components and accessories were assembled in four groups. The large transmitter positioned on a semi-cylindrical stand was affixed to the floor against the cabin. A worktable that held all the other radio components took its place sideways on the left of the main body; it was fully pre-wired, with a work lamp, plug, and a small electric heater. The wall storage on the right-hand side served as storage for various components, like tuning units, coil units and spare batteries. The fourth group was a seat/chest to store materials such as lamps, quartz, antennae and baseplates.

The electricity supply was provided by a PE-95 generator, which delivered—from a gasoline engine

Fort Leonard Wood, Missouri, January 27, 1942. This member of the 162nd Signal Photographic Company prepares the emulsions he will need in the campaign dark room that is his panel G-7105-NG, registration number 356779. (U.S. Army SC-133335)

Myitkyina Aerodrome, Burma, in late 1944. Major Theodore G. Dominy, Intelligence and Commanding Officer of the 17th Photographic Intelligence Unit, gives instructions to the pilots of the 9th Photographic Reconnaissance Group, Tenth U.S. Army Air Force. Note the Chevrolet panel delivery behind them. (U.S. Army Air Forces A-26233)

A K-51 radio vehicle at the Amphibious Training Center, Camp Gordon Johnston, Florida, February 23, 1943. (U.S. Army SC-257527)

similar to a Willys Jeep—a power of 5 to 10 kW depending on its configuration, for an alternative current of 110 to 240 volts. It was set up in a 1-ton-type trailer. In this specific case, the whole rig was referenced as K-52 by the Signal Corps. The specially fitted trailer was also equipped with a permanent supply line towards the truck, six jerry cans of five gallons each and a storage trunk.

CENSUS OF REGISTRATIONS ALLOCATED TO PANEL DELIVERY TRUCKS

Contract	Year	Body Type	Registration	Total Units
W-398-QM-8278	1940	YP-G 4112-YG panel delivery	(W-328401 to W-328442) (W-331684 to W-331695)	54
W-398-QM-9402	1941	ZP-G 4105-ZG panel delivery	(W-337301 to W-337446)	146
W-398-QM-10328	1941	G-7105-NG	(347683 to 347704) (353189 to 353228) (348821 to 348840)	86
W-398-QM-10912	1942	G-7105-NG	(356736 to 356915)	180
W-398-QM-10510	1942	G-7105-NG	(3106797 to 3107021) (3103417 to 3103813) (3105514 to 3105654) (3218879 to 3219063) (3219064 to 3219284)	1,546 units and 376 units with no registration number for the Navy and the U.S. Marine Corps
W-398-QM-11546	1942	G-7105-NG	(365531 to 365747)	217
W-398-QM-12396	1942	G-7105-NG	(370051 to 370730) (3114813 to 3115462)	1,330
DA-W-398-QM-8	1942	G-7105-NG	No registration number	180
DA-W-398-QM-421	1942	G-7105-NG	No registration number	220
DA-W-398-QM-243	1942	G-7105-NG	No registration number	75

Left and below: Fresh from the assembly line, panel delivery K-51 G-7105-NG's ID from the Signal Corps, at the Desert Training Center, June 8, 1942. The vehicle is presented here with a full range of options, with all antennae in place. (U.S. Army SC-141581/141582)

The bulk created by all these accessories on the side of the panel delivery, necessitated the removal of the spare wheel bracket to the inside of the trailer. However, during campaigns, it became so cumbersome that the crew would move it underneath the trailer until this position was officially implemented.

Being part of the larger units' communications hub, the K-51/K-52 was responsible for facilitating intercommunication between senior commands to coordinate operations. They also allowed interconnection to the telephone network. The two phone cable side reels as well as the two portable phone posts tucked away under the worktable, allowed the SCR-299 to work from a distance.

The K-51 in Action

With the SCR-299 set up in a Chevrolet panel delivery, long-distance communications in operational theaters became much easier, and it was in North Africa, during the landings of Operation *Torch* in November 1942, that the K-51 made its debut. The 829th Signal Service Battalion ensured coordination between the various forces involved in the operation, via the main command post at Gibraltar. During the campaign, the K-51s accompanied the advancing troops and gave military communications such a boost that General Dwight Eisenhower praised their essential contribution. Later, they helped in a similar fashion in Sicily and Italy.

Right: The cramped interior of a K-51 equipped with an SCR-299, with even a large storage trunk under the operators' bench seat. (U.S. Army SC-174435)

Below: August 18, 1944, Caserta, Italy. T/5 Irving Katsper transmits from the SCR-299 installed in a panel K-51. Note the numerous Signal Corps markings stenciled on the inside of the rear door, which concern the specifications of the transceiver. (U.S. Army SC-198634)

Side view of panel delivery G-7105-NG at a Signal Corps depot. The vehicle is still to be delivered to its unit and has no markings apart from the registration number done at the factory. (U.S. Army Signal Corps)

View of the 60th Signal Operation Battalion's bivouac on Leyte Island in the Philippines. Two Chevrolet radios are in operating position under the palm trees. Two trailers with generators can be seen in the foreground. (U.S. Army SC-255877)

Near Bristol, England, the 56th Signal Battalion on maneuvers, January 27, 1943. Its K-51s were the backbone of V Corps' communications. (U.S. Army SC-174436)

This K-51 from the 21st Signal Battalion, Third U.S. Army Air Force, is towing a Jeep, the location unknown. (U.S. Army Signal Corps)

This transport is leaving the United States for the Pacific, with most of the vehicles belonging to the Signal Corps. Amidst the CCKW-353 K-53s, 1-ton trailers, and CCK-W353 Signal Repair Ordnance trucks M-30, Chevrolet G-7105-NG panel delivery trucks can be seen. (U.S. Army Signal Corps)

Djebinina, Tunisia, May 9, 1943. The electric cable between the PE-95 generator and the truck is visible; note also the unofficial placement of the spare wheel under the trailer. (U.S. Army SC-380488)

The 102nd Infantry Division at Camp Maxey, Texas, in 1942, with a Signal Company K-51 in action. The interior of the panel is barely big enough to fit the equipment and two operators. (Private collection)

During the early days of the Normandy invasion, the K-51 was the only quick method of communication between war correspondents and Britain.

In the Pacific, the Marine Corps took its K-51s all the way to Japan, but the days of the Chevy panel radio were numbered. Too awkward and too cumbersome for sea travel, its replacement was already on its way. From November 1942, a study was made for the realization of a special body—a 'shelter'—that could be installed on a standard chassis. Thus the Shelter HO-17 line was born. The SCR-299 post survived the K-51's disappearance: in its Shelter-specific and updated form, it became the SCR-399, whilst in its simplified airborne use, it would be labelled SCR-499.

January 18, 1943 at Youks-les-bains, Algeria. A K-51 Chevy is set up in a protective trench. The camouflage consists of netting and a layer of soil on the roof. (U.S. Army Air Forces A-27766)

5 Cargo Dump Trucks

15,946 vehicles of two different models made up this category of 145-inch short-wheelbase dump trucks.

The differences between a cargo and a cargo dump are near impossible to tell from this angle, but closer inspection reveals a control lever for the tailgate and the absence of mudguards over the twin wheels. This G-7116-NL is an early third-series model. (U.S. Army Signal Corps)

Included in this number, 10,008 were winchless cargo dump trucks (1,558 G-4112s, 1,384 G-4152s, and 7,066 G-7106s), and 5,938 were cargo dumps with winch (284 G-4112s, 500 G-4162s, and 5,154 G-7116s). The figures from Defense Aid and Lend-Lease account for 669 units delivered to Allied countries, though there are unfortunately no details on the specific models supplied.

The designation of the vehicle requires little in the way of explanation. It was a truck with a tipping dumpster, that could take soil, sand, gravel, coal, etc. The technical component was composed of a metallic platform with three drop-sides and five arches to hold the canvas roofing. The lateral drop-sides were made with a rotating function to become bench seats when the vehicle was used to transport troops. At first glance, it looked like the short-wheelbase cargo truck;

The same machine with the dumpster fully elevated. The double faux chassis is visible here and allows the easy tipping of the body. (U.S. Army Signal Corps)

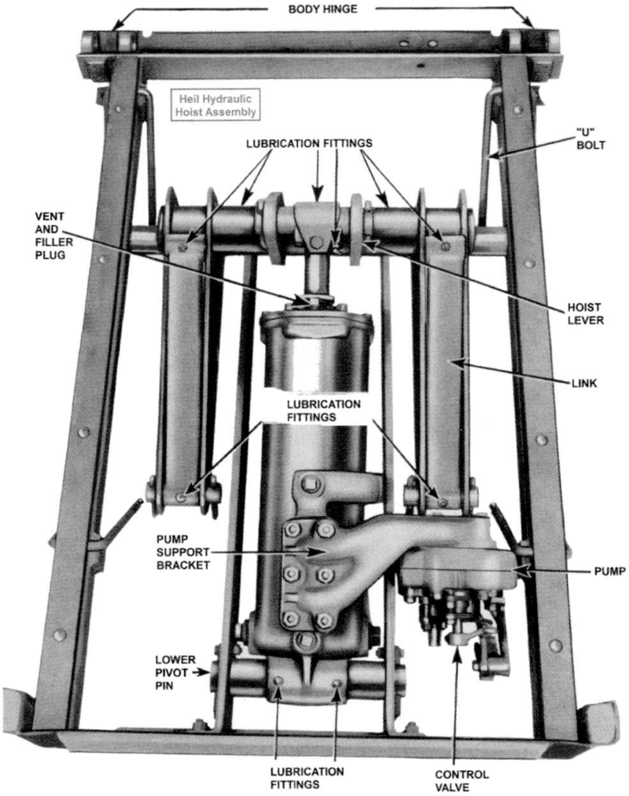

Above: The technical aspects of the cargo dump G-4112 are characteristic, with the triangular side reinforcements and the arches fitting into flanges. (Extract fromTM 10-1438)

Above and below: Although based on one concept, the hydraulic parts of the dumpster's lifting mechanism were not interchangeable, as each manufacturer—Hercules, Heil, or Perfection—had its own features; this at a time when the army was standardizing as many elements as possible. (Extracts from TM 10-1127 and 10-1557)

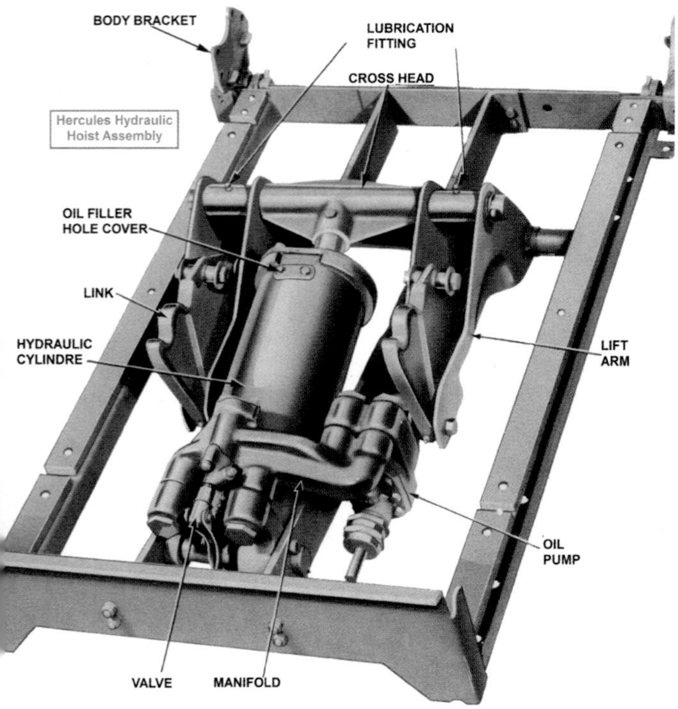

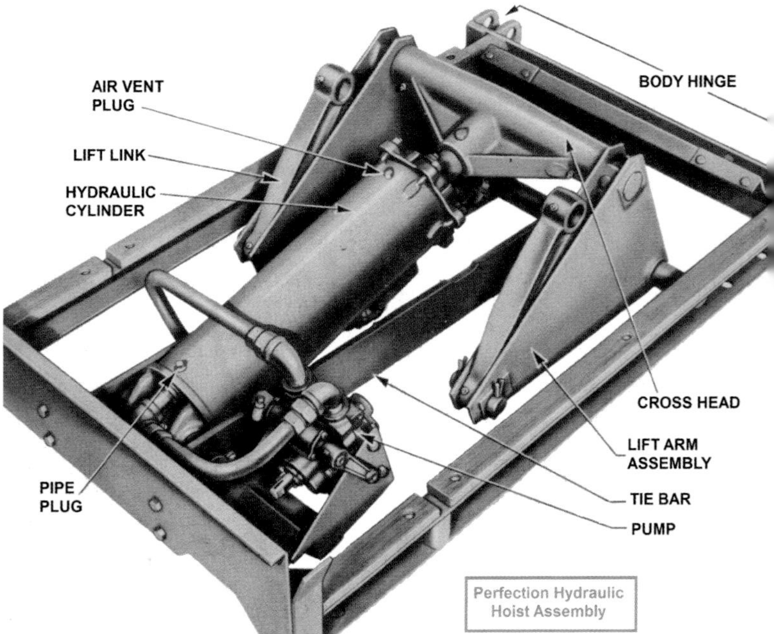

however, its dimensions were slightly different at 110½ x 86 inches, with an inside width of 66 inches, a loss of 20 inches due to the width of the sides. Curiously, the arches were 62½ inches high, 3½ inches higher than simple cargo trucks.

The Dumpster

During the entire production run, the dumpster remained fully metallic, but it changed drastically after the first 1,842 units of the G-4112 series were delivered. In the first version, each side was reinforced by large triangular structures and the three central arches were kept in place solely by two flanges. Later, the external aspect became identical to the cargo version, all arches were attached with a sheath and the triangular reinforcements disappeared. It was also at that time that the rear suspension was reinforced, adding a set of leaf springs above the original.

Above: Cleaning time for these two Chevy cargo dumps. In the foreground is a winchless YP-G 4112-YH with an early body design. In the background is a ZP-G 4162-ZL with winch. The canvases indicate that they have just returned from transporting troops. (Private collection)

Right: Used in large numbers during the construction of the Alcan Highway, cargo dumps were hammered as the second vehicle in this photo shows. The rear view of the one in the foreground gives a good perspective of the position of the lights on the longerons. (U.S. Army Signal Corps)

CENSUS OF REGISTRATIONS ALLOCATED TO WINCHLESS CARGO DUMP TRUCKS				
Contract	**Year**	**Body Type**	**Registration**	**Total Units**
W-398-QM-8278	1940	YP-G 4112-YH winchless	(W-327058 to W-328025) (W-330966 to W-331555)	1,558
W-398-QM-9402	1941	ZP-G 4152-ZH winchless	(W-335887 to W-337270) [1]	1,384
W-398-QM-9402	1941	G-7106-NH	(337271 to 337300)	30
W-398-QM-10328	1941	G-7106-NH	(347443 to 347642) (348761 to 348810) (349460 to 349709) (350514 to 350713) (351619 to 351718) (352974 to 353173) (357616 to 357650) (358551 to 358615) (359141 to 359190) [2]	2,150
W-398-QM-11510	1942	G-7106-NH	(398928 to 399999) (3100000 to 3101873) (3121234 to 3123173)	4,886

Notes:

1. 30 of these trucks were converted to G-7133-NZ fire trucks
2. Add a further 1,000 units with no registration numbers for the Navy and the U.S.M.C.

To these 10,008 winchless cargo dumps can be added 104 bare chassis units converted to cargo dump trucks by the Hercules Company in 1945.

In this specific case and for an accurate description, it is necessary to note the name of two manufacturers. Although not considered as being supplied by the Edw. G. Budd Manufacturing Company, the bodies of these dump trucks did come from there and passed through—at least administratively—the jacking mechanism's manufacturer. There were three of these specialists for the G-7000 series: Hercules Steel Products, with its K.D.O. model, the Heil Company (SL-1 model) and Perfection Steel Body Company (615-Special model). A power takeoff from Gar Wood Industries (model 69y9000CD-Rey) or Spicer

Guadalcanal, December 8, 1942. The compact size of the vehicle was an asset in the amphibious operation, as it could easily fit onto an L.C.M. craft to bring immediate logistic support ashore. (US Army SC-164895)

Manufacturing Company (model YAC7M) activated the mechanism. Both models were of double type when the truck had a winch. For winchless trucks, the P.T.O. was single, supplied by Central Fiber Products Company (model 2-B-13).

The dumpster rested on a double faux chassis, articulated at the rear with a hydraulic actuator and pump. The body was controlled by two levers located in the cabin: the first was an on/off switch that started or stopped the activation of the P.T.O. and the second activated the hydraulic valve that controlled the jacking mechanism.

Above: November 23, 1943, the 165th Infantry Regiment has just landed on Butaritari, Makin Atoll, with a G-7106-NH from the Engineers Corps. (U.S. Army SC-183549)

Right: May 1, 1943, England. A team of Air Force firefighters are repairing a runway. This G-7106-NH has just delivered a fresh load of concrete. (U.S. Army Air Forces 79181.A.C.)

CENSUS OF REGISTRATIONS ALLOCATED TO CARGO DUMP TRUCKS WITH WINCH				
Contract	**Year**	**Body Type**	**Registration**	**Total Units**
W-398-QM-8278	1941	YP-G 4112-YL with winch	(W-328026 to W-328309)	284
W-398-QM-9402	1941	ZP-G 4162-ZL with winch	(W-337447 to W-337945) W-332065	500
W-398-QM-10328	1941	G-7116-NL	(347643 to 347682) (348811 to 348820) (349710 to 349728) (350714 to 350768) (351719 to 351768) (353174 to 353188) (358616 to 358640) (359191 to 359215) 353243	250
W-398-QM-10939	1942	G-7116-NL	(362127 to 362626	500
W-398-QM-11510	1942	G-7116-NL	(3103814 to 3105513) (3101884 to 3103416)	4,038 units and 805 units with no registration numbers for the Navy and the U.S.M.C.
DA-W-398-QM-8	1942	G-7116-NL	No registration number	350
DA-W-398-QM-171	1942	G-7116-NL	No registration number	16

On the hills overlooking Anzio Bay, the Allies have opened a hospital. In the foreground Engineers are attending to ruined buildings with a cable and a Chevrolet G-7116-NL. (U.S. Navy)

Above: July 7, 1943, Molesworth, England. The registration number of this vehicle identifies it as a G-7116-NL. Note the Perfection brand hydraulic system. At the front of the dumpster the tailgate lever is horizontal, which means the opening mechanism can be reached when the dumpster is elevated. (U.S. Army Air Forces 79553.A.C.)

Left: March 1943, Algeria. U.S. troops are attending to the aerodrome at Maison Blanche d'Alger. Earth and grass runways soon made way for concrete ones. After laying down a base of large aggregates, the Chevys then unloaded a layer of smaller stones before finishing and smoothing it all with concrete. (U.S. Army Air Forces 23487.A.C.)

Right: May 12, 1943, the 96th Engineer Combat Battalion, 41st Infantry Division conducting road maintenance in New Guinea. As was often the case the drop-sides have been removed to make for easier loading and unloading. Here, unloading is done with the tailgate swiveling on the bottom axle. (U.S. Army SC-182575)

Below: Cargo dumps (with winch) waiting at the quayside at the port of Nouméa, New Caledonia, for a contingent of G.I.s to disembark. Their multifunctional capacity did not limit them to civil engineering work. (U.S. Army SC-172461)

Camp Robinson, Arkansas, December 16, 1941. Private First Class Paul Turner lost control of his YP-G 4112-YH, which crashed into Miss Louanna Miller's Chevrolet 40. The cargo dump belonged to the 43rd Engineer Combat Battalion and the civilian vehicle to the Baptist Church. (U.S. Army SC-133426)

Whilst the overall design of this dumpster could be likened to the cargo version, it differed in various ways at the rear: it was lower due to the absence of the storage trunk, and the location of the lights on brackets affixed to the chassis. The hatchback was articulated on two separate horizontal axes. The first, of a traditional concept, articulated the panel on a low axis that rotated towards the ground, just like a normal cargo body; the second, with its high axis, was controlled by a lever located on the front right-hand side, accessible from the running board, which allowed the driver to open the back without having to go all the way around the truck. This second option allowed the unloading of aggregates without damaging the hatchback. Note that this body had no protective partition at the front, nor any cabin protection or mudguard.

June 20, 1942, these YP-G 4112-YHs are being washed in an Icelandic lake. One of the driver's duties was to keep on top of basic maintenance; outside combat zones, inspections were performed daily and having dirty equipment was not an option. (U.S. Army SC-142656)

Large-scale maneuvers, October 1941, North Carolina. This YP-G 4112 belonging to the First Army is unloading P.S.P. plates for runway construction of. From this angle it is impossible to determine if the vehicle is equipped with a winch. (U.S. Army SC-125542)

Large-scale maneuvers, September 1942, Louisiana. This cargo dump G-7106-NH is crossing a river on a pontoon. Eight paddlers are guiding the raft. (Associated Press Photo PO-1199)

Too Small but Ideal for the Pacific Islands

Created during peacetime, these small-sized cargo-dump 1½-ton, 4x4s were promptly replaced with 2½-ton, 6x6 vehicles and their production was stopped in 1943. Yet they would participate in titanic works and were pretty much the only cargo dump trucks available during the construction of the famous Alcan Highway. This channel was opened in 1942 to link the United States and Alaska via Canada, during the invasion of the Aleutian Islands by Japanese troops in June of the same year.

With the appearance of the General Motors CCKW-353 H1, H2, and L1, the Chevrolet cargo dump trucks were relegated to secondary tasks, though they remained in the engineering units' fleet. Initially in the Pacific, on all the islands where landing could be hazardous, only barges could be relied upon to deliver matériel. Chevys and particularly cargo dumps readily found their place on board Landing Craft Mechanized (L.C.M.s), which together with the Landing Craft Vehicle & Personnel (L.C.V.P.s), were the first vessels to land. The engineering troops who had to be up and running quickly continued to favor the Chevrolet despite its more diminutive format.

Barely arrived, these men from the 8th Engineers Pontoon Battalion are testing their bridge and the Chevy cargo dumps are the first to try it out. As was often the case, the wide rims on the side of the body were used for storage; here they are fitted with toolboxes. (U.S. Army SC-120124)

6 Tractor Trucks

Only one model of this tractor was present in the order books, with a total of 3,530 vehicles.

These were fifth-wheel coupling trucks with the 145-inch short wheelbase, but only 2,943 of them were for the U.S. Army, 587 of them seeing their orders cancelled. There were eight G-4112s, 89 G-4165s, and 2,846 G-7113s. Forty-nine units were allocated to Allied nations through Defense Aid and Lend-Lease.

Tractor trucks, which could be confused with bare chassis vehicles, were specific to the U.S. Army. They occupied a niche that developed at the end of the 1930s, when two primary ideas prevailed. The first advocated the physical separation between the mechanical and technical parts, veering strongly towards trailers

The first YP-G-4112-YK tractor trucks were very understated, with no spare wheel and no toolbox on the longeron. This model is towing an old cartographic trailer. (U.S. Army Signal Corps)

February 13, 1945, Motor Pool at the Holabird Signal Depot, Baltimore, Maryland. G-7113 tractor trucks are lined in anticipation of their delivery to their allocated units. Note the reconnaissance stars on top of the cabins, as per Army Regulation 850-5 of August 5, 1942. Not all models are equipped with the blackout drive kit; those that are have it superimposed on the grille near the left-hand headlamp. (U.S. Army Signal Corps)

Right: Despite their limited numbers, ZP-G-4165-ZK tractor trucks have reached maturity in their design. The leaf springs at the rear have been doubled and a spare wheel support has been installed behind the cabin. (U.S. Army Signal Corps)

Below: September 13, 1945, the U.S. Navy also used Chevrolet tractors; this model is towing a trailer being used as a bus. Arriving from Guam, the USS *Ozark* (LSV-2) has just docked in the Mariana Islands, with 970 recently freed prisoners of war on board. (U.S. Navy)

September 4, 1944, tractor trucks from the 3814th Truck Company, Advance Section Communication Zone. Before loading, each driver had to check the overall condition of his vehicle and ensure fuel levels were adequate. Each depot had an area reserved for this purpose. (U.S. Army SC-193665)

and semi-trailers. The theory was supported by considerations of practical use. In the case of a full truck breaking down, it was not only the driving element that came to a halt, but also the technical element of the truck. Vice-versa, when the technical element needed maintenance, the whole vehicle was out of order, which meant there was always a large risk of immobilization.

CENSUS OF REGISTRATIONS ALLOCATED TO TRACTOR TRUCKS

Contract	Year	Body Type	Registration	Total Units
W-398-QM-8278	1941	YP-G 4112-YK tractor	(W-328761 to W-328768)	8
W-398-QM-9402	1941	ZP-G 4165-ZK tractor	(W-337946 to W-338034)	89
W-398-QM-10328	1942	G-7113-NK	(347708 to 347740) (353229 to 353242) 352783	48
W-398-QM-10939	1942	G-7113-NK	No registration number	44
W-398-QM-11510	1942	G-7113-NK	(3105655 to 3106796) (3107022 to 3107123) (3219499 to 3220099) (3296276 to 3297496) [1]	3,066
W-398-QM-12980	1942	G-7113-NK	(3109758 to 3109883)	126
W-374-ORD-018-517	1944	G-7113-NK	(3434454 to 3434578) [2]	125
DA-W-398-QM-8	1942	G-7113-NK	No registration number	24

Notes:

1. 462 units were removed from this order
2. Order cancelled

2,943 out of the 3,530 units ordered were received by the Ordnance Department.

According to the Ordnance Department Administrative and Tactical Vehicles Report of October 1, 1945, the following 587 registration numbers were not used: 3297035 to 3297496 and 3434454 to 3434578.

Fort Monmouth, April 24, 1942. This tractor truck is towing a trailer type K-55 from the Signal Corps. (U.S. Army SC-133821)

June 30, 1944, this convoy of Chevrolet G-7113s has just loaded up combat supplies at a depot near Cherbourg and is heading out towards Chartres. (U.S. Army SC-210067)

August 22, 1944, Leyte Island, Philippines. Despite all the vehicles having chains on their wheels, unloading vehicles was always difficult on the Pacific beaches. This Chevy and its 3-ton semi-trailer van need some external help. (U.S. Army Signal Corps)

Above: July 1944, Carentan area. Just arrived in Cherbourg, material from the 5th General Hospital is being unloaded from a G-7113. (U.S. Army Signal Corps)

Right: This well-known photograph—the location of which is uncertain though it could be the Cherbourg depot mentioned earlier—shows a typical convoy size. (U.S. Army SC-193666)

Left: Supply lines were shortened as soon the railways became operational, but road transport continued to play a part; a mixed system was set up which reduced delivery waiting times by half. (U.S. Army Signal Corps)

Below: A G-7113 leaving a fuel depot in Reims. Its trailer has been simplified: the drop-sides have been removed to transport a water tank. This was one of the many ways these 3½-ton (6-ton gross) S&P semi-trailers could be used—one day as a cargo, the next as a simple flatbed trailer. (U.S. Army Signal Corps)

1941 on the Alaska Highway, a curious customized trailer attached to a tractor truck, for the transport of excessively long objects, in this case piping of sorts. (Private collection)

June 27, 1944, Cherbourg has just been liberated and the first supplies are being unloaded. The port is not as yet serviceable, so DUKWs and Chevy tractor truck G-7113s (there are five of them visible on this photo) shuttle between the ships and the shore. (U.S. Army SC-209664)

The second theory was for compact and non-separable vehicles, supported by strategic considerations. In the case of frontline military operations, when on the move it was easier to operate with vehicles that formed a single unit. Not having to hitch and unhitch trailers gained precious time during a withdrawal, for example. It also ensured that all mechanical and technical elements were always together.

Both theories were insular and failed to consider the other's imperatives. In the end, what prevailed in the U.S. Army was a mix of the two, a line that differentiated between tactics and strategy, the front and the lines of communication: the front and its immediate rear were allocated fully integrated trucks, and the other military zones, safer and more easily accessible overall, were afforded tractors and semi-trailers.

It was in this optic that the 1½-ton, 4x4 Chevrolet tractor truck was born, evolving into semi-trailer tractors with electric brakes and 7.5x20 tires. These trailers were mostly divided into three categories, the first specific to the Signal Corps with vans and electronic gear platforms, like the K-55 or K-67 trailers, for example. The other two categories were originally defined by the Quartermaster Corps, and later the Ordnance Department, with 3-ton van semi-trailers, (6-ton gross), and 3½-ton stake and platform (S&P) drop-side trailers (6-ton gross), both single axle and twin wheeled.

The tractor truck line evolved from the initial three principal production series. The first G-4112 tractors were very simplified vehicles, and it wasn't until the G-4165 that the spare wheel, trunk, and rear suspension reinforcements made their appearances.

Similar to the rest of the line, the tractor truck G-7113 differed however in several essential ways: the technical element comprised a spare wheel located across the chassis, right behind the cabin, a storage trunk affixed along the left longeron and a fifth-wheel coupling for securing the semi-trailer's swivel. The latter, contrary to the G-4112 and G-4165, became very specific. On the first two series, the fifth-wheel coupling was a traditional single articulation, fit for absorbing light front/back tilting movements; on the G-7113, due to the all-terrain nature of the vehicle, it changed to a double articulation, thereby allowing lateral movement.

The CS&P (Combination Stake & Platform) semi-trailer. Once its drop-sides were removed, it became a large working surface. Add a few accessories and it could carry very large items, in this instance Waco CG-4A glider wings. (U.S. Army Air Forces)

An essential part of the tractor trucks was the double-axle fifth wheel. This particularity made the G-7113 a vehicle perfectly suited to supply missions whatever the driving conditions. (Extract TM)

The trailer's electric braking system was activated by simple pressure on the vehicle brake pedal to which it was connected via an extra rod, the trailer electric brake control. The mechanical movement connected with a range of strips that transmitted electric pulses necessary to operate the trailer's brakes. To ensure adequate braking depending on the load of the trailer, or even the difficulty of the terrain to traverse, the electric charge was modifiable, via a dial on the

Left: Luxembourg, January 25, 1945, at a XIX Tactical Air Command radar station. The G-7113 is attached to a K-55 semi-trailer van, although K-67 semi-trailers could also be used for the same purpose. The Signal Corps was a primary user of the Chevrolet tractor truck, and several of its trailers were calibrated for it. (U.S. Army Air Forces B.61310-AC)

Below: Another view of the beach at Cherbourg with similar vehicles. The short distances to the inland depots meant that the 2½-ton trucks and the 1½-ton tractors were more flexible than larger machines like the 4- or 5-ton tractor, for example. (U.S. Army SC-209670)

dashboard, the trailer electric brake load control. Progressing from 1 to 4, it allowed for a light to heavy action on the trailer's brakes.

The 1½-ton, 4x4 Chevrolet tractor truck was an unobtrusive vehicle, mostly noted for its wide-scale use during crucial supply missions in 1944. The Red Ball Express route was one example where it demonstrated its flexibility and maneuverability.

Semi-Trailers

Three main types of semi-trailers were designed to be towed by the 1½-ton, 4x4 Chevrolet tractor truck. These were all-purpose vans, removable drop-side trailers, and special trailers for the Signal Corps, which amounted to 4,239 trailers.

As was customary, the U.S. Army calibrated its trailers in accordance with its tractors; for example, the 7.5x20 tires of both tractor and trailer were of the same dimensions: the spare wheel of one could thus be used on either element. These semi-trailers were all equipped with electric brakes, which accounts for the technical elements necessary for these types of brakes being located in the cabin.

Right and below: The S&P 3½-ton (6-ton gross) semi-trailer was one of the two principal trailers towed by the Chevy. This model photographed at the Holabird Quartermaster Depot on December 10, 1941 was made by the Winter Weiss Company. The rear view shows the various components that made up the removable drop-sides which allowed conversion to a flatbed, held in place by vertical stands and latches at the top corners. (U.S. Army SC-127218 et SC-127219)

Below: A K-55 semi-trailer van in operational position, all panels open. Here it is equipped with an SCR-698 for trials at the Signal Corps General Development Laboratory, Fort Monmouth, December 26, 1942. (U.S. Army SC-148338)

Stake and Platform 3½-ton (6-ton gross) Semi-Trailer

These were produced by ten different companies, which shared 20 contracts for a total production of 1,818 units. Its peculiarity was that it was modular: it was both a cargo when its 11 panels were in place, and a flatbed when they were dismantled. The latter configuration allowed a multitude of loading options, especially when used with trestles to support large or lengthy pieces of equipment.

3-ton (6-ton gross) Semi-Trailer Van

This model was manufactured by nine companies, of which six also delivered the S&P model as above. Twenty-one orders were delivered to the U.S. Army, for a total of 2,296 vans. In theory, these were all

Below: The 3-ton (6-ton gross) semi-trailer van was the second standard model to be towed by G-7113s. These were used to transport loads that needed protection from the elements. (U.S. Army SC-127222)

classified as 3 ton, but some manufacturers, for ease of production, made no differentiation between the base of the two models and produced 3½-ton vans.

Using both wood and steel, they permitted transport of all kinds of material, but required specific protection. Five of these trailer models were destined for the Chemical Warfare Service and were partitioned for the transport of special munitions.

1½-ton Semi-Trailer Van K-55

Delivered by two manufacturers, with four orders for 125 units, these double-axle trailers were working spaces, mostly used for long-range radio installations, or U.S. Army Air Forces radar control posts.

Medical Trailers

Only seven were produced in 1942. These were 2½-ton, 4-wheel surgical van semi-trailers, which also needed the Chevrolet tractor truck to move them. The rapid development of the medical field meant that this type was replaced with various models based on the General Motors CCKW-353.

Right: December 10, 1941, the back view of the van, with two side-opening doors for optimal closure and protection of the load. (U.S. Army SC-127223)

Below: A 1942 photograph of a tractor truck type ZP-G-4165-ZK, recognizable by the lack of fuel filter on the side of the right longeron. It is towing an old 2½-ton map-reproduction equipment van trailer. (Private collection)

7 Bomb Service Truck M6

A very specific vehicle in the 1½-ton, 4x4 Chevrolet line, the bomb service truck M6 saw 11,992 units ordered under the reference G-7128-NQ. Only 8,459 were received by the Air Force, the order for the other 3,533 having been cancelled.

Eighty-five of these trucks were delivered as part of the Lend-Lease agreement, and a further 736 were allocated to the U.S. Navy and Marine Corps, though with a bare chassis, and no rear equipment. Other than their very specific design, the 125-inch wheelbase was another of the characteristics.

Left: The 341st Bombardment Group, somewhere in India. The distance between depot and aircraft was sometimes significant. Here a bomb service M6, part of a convoy, is on its way to deliver bombs to B-25 bombers. (U.S. Army Air Forces A-66950-AC)

Below: Handling 1,000-lb. bombs on Ngeaur Island in the Carolina Archipelago, November 1944. This view highlights the squat aspect of this truck. The leaf springs are fastened at the end of the longerons and the truck has no bumper. (U.S. Army Air Forces A-64210-AC)

Concept

The concept for this kind of machine goes back to 1939 when the U.S. Army Air Forces were researching a vehicle that could handle bombs at aviation facilities. It had to be light, so as to be able to drive around ammunition depots and without a cabin that might restrict a driver's vision in such dangerous conditions. The idea of an aero-transportable truck was still some way off. It only had to be able to load and unload trailers, and transport bombs between the depot and the apron or runway.

Marmon-Herrington was the first to manufacture the machine that the Army would call the T1 bomb service. Later on, Ford built a few dozen units, based on its 19Y model, a 4x2 ½-ton; General Motors joined in with a 1-ton chassis model AC-251 in 1940. In 1941, Diamond T delivered 136 units of the 201-BS 4x2 1½-ton; Ford produced an unknown number of them on a 1½-ton chassis. All these would be referred to as the bomb service truck M1.

As with most matériel, military rationing was in effect and Chevrolet was asked to look through its specifications to produce a bomb service truck on its 1½-ton, 4x4 truck chassis. The standardization

Above: Saint-Pierre-du-Mont, Normandy. The M6 could also be used for other tasks like transporting a spare tank for this Republic P-47. The airfield has just been commissioned thanks to the 834th Aviation Engineers Battalion. (Army Signal Corps)

Left: The M6 manual winch. (Private collection)

of what became the bomb service truck M6 was presented on July 10, 1941 and approved a few weeks later on August 14. Curiously though, the earliest purchase orders were dated 1943. By February 1944, the decision to interrupt production was made and put into effect by September. Rapid aircraft development meant that the Chevrolet had become too small and the bomb service M27, on the inevitable 2½-ton, 6x6 General Motors chassis made its debut.

Right: Saipan Island, Mariana Archipelago, September 6, 1944. The 1-ton bomb lift in action, loading a 1,000-lb. bomb. This particular model has been modified so ordnance can be lifted higher. (U.S. Army Air Forces A-54619-AC)

Below: The bomb trailer M5 had the distinctive feature of being configured as a train. These trailers have longitudinal suspensions and are loaded with 500-lb. bombs. The trailers are being loaded manually with the help of ramps. (U.S. Army Air Forces A-54620-AC)

Design

Despite a smaller chassis and shorter wheelbase, the bomb service truck M6 was a fully-fledged 1½-ton, 4x4 Chevrolet in its mechanical aspects. It was not equipped with a winch, it did not have a spare wheel, nor twin back wheels. The cabin had two seats, each with armrests to avoid falls, and its windshield was a single piece. As they were only meant to travel on air bases, they were originally fitted with a simple 18-gallon tank located under the cabin. But this quickly proved to be too small and a second tank of 30 gallons was positioned under the technical elements, between the two longerons. Swapping over fuel tanks was triggered by a lever on the cabin floor, by the passenger's feet. The fuel gauge, being common to both tanks, allowed the individual reading of each tank via a changeover switch

The absence of a cabin allowed the driver more maneuverability and enhanced peripheral vision, which was needed to navigate ammunition depots. (U.S. Army Air Forces A-49613-AC)

India, February 10, 1945. Loading bombs on P-47s of the 1st Air Commando Group. With no back to the cabin and no frame around the windshield, the driver's view is a full 360°. (U.S. Army Air Forces A-72730-AC)

Ascension Island, July 30, 1943. The M5 was not limited to transporting bombs: it also carried other loads as seen here with crates of ammunition destined for aircraft machine guns. (U.S. Army Air Forces A-54620-AC)

February 7, 1945, India. Loading Boeing B-29s of the 468th Bomb Group. The rear view of the M5 trailer shows the tow hook for another trailer and a plug for connecting the electrics. (U.S. Army Air Forces A-66450-AC)

Suspended from an M6 gantry is a 55-gallon incendiary bomb, being installed by men of the Chemical Warfare Service inside this consolidated B-24. (U.S. Army Air Forces A-66450-AC)

CENSUS OF REGISTRATIONS ALLOCATED TO BOMB SERVICE TRUCKS M6				
Contract	**Year**	**Body Type**	**Registration**	**Total Units**
W-374-ORD-1131	1941	G-7128-NQ	(004373 to 004863)	491
W-374-ORD-1185	1942	G-7128-NQ	(006070 to 006185) (006186 to 006312)	243
W-374-ORD-1281	1942	G-7128-NQ	(007987 to 008421)	435
W-374-ORD-1580	1942	G-7128-NQ	(0012010 to 0012555) 0012557	547
W-374-ORD-2216	1943	G-7128-NQ	(0022800 to 0024500)	1,701
W-374-ORD-4052	1943	G-7128-NQ	(0036252 to 0038610)	2,359
W-374-ORD-5051	1943	G-7128-NQ	(0061361 to 0063484) [1]	2,124
W-374-ORD-6072	1944	G-7128-NQ	(0068534 to 0071889) [2]	3,356
W-374-ORD-6072	1944	G-7128-NQ	No registration number [3]	736

Notes:

1. 177 units were removed from this order
2. Order cancelled
3. For the Navy and the U.S.M.C. bare chassis with open cabin and no rear equipment

According to the Department Administrative and Tactical Vehicles Report of October 1, 1945, the following 3,533 registration numbers were not used: 0063308 to 0063484 and 0068534 to 0071889.

The rear part was made of a wooden platform that articulated on a load-lifting gantry, on which was installed a 2,000-lb manual winch. On the left-hand running board was a side trunk that accommodated various tools.

Behind the cabin was a transversal trunk for the apparatus necessary for various maneuvers. Leaning on the back on the lifting structure, was a three-seater trunk for the extra crew needed during the loading of munitions onto the aircraft. If the vehicle was equipped with a pioneer tool rack, it would be affixed to the back of that seat. The space available under the gantry was used to store the bomb lift M1, which was used to affix ordnance under the wings of fighter-bombers.

Saipan Island, November 1944. M6s were also used to rearrange ammunition depots. The bombing campaign against Japan necessitated a vast array of bombs. (U.S. Army Air Forces A-64244-AC)

The crew of this bomb service truck takes a break from loading a Boeing B-29 Superfortress. (U.S. Army Air Forces A-64303-AC)

December 1944, Ninth Air Force base, Belgium. As well as the risks involved during missions from enemy fighters or flak, pilots also had to contend with weather conditions that could be disastrous. Ice on the runway caused this P-38 Lightning to crash into four M6 bomb service trucks and M5 bomb trailers. (U.S. Army Air Forces A-55556-AC)

Above: Guam, Mariana Archipelago, September 9, 1944. To increase the maneuverability of the truck and avoid sideways movement, a lifting device was affixed to the gantry that could rotate 180°. (U.S. Army Air Forces A-56511-AC)

Right: An Engineer Aviation Fire Fighting Platoon is trying to put out a fire. Equipped with a knapsack sprayer, a G.I. sprays foam. An inadequate piece of equipment, it had to be topped up often to have any impact on a blaze. (U.S. Army Air Forces A-55544-AC)

Winter 1944, France. To protect themselves against the weather this bomb service M6 crew has constructed a cabin made of planks of wood and paneling. This non-regulatory addition gave them a modicum of comfort, despite hindering visibility. (Army Signal Corps)

Customization

If ever there was a vehicle that did not please all its users, it was the bomb service M6. The gantry's manual winch, manufactured by Beebe, very quickly showed excessive signs of wear and tear, and frequently jammed. To such an extent that Chevrolet quickly proceeded to replace it on the assembly lines with a mechanism produced by Holan. By May 18, 1943, all the vehicles already supplied to the U.S. Army were sent a replacement kit with a Braden manual winch to be installed. However, it was often the basis of the concept that was put into question, the use of a manual winch required a lot of strength and the sole lifting function was deemed too restrictive; it meant a lot of maneuvers to load and unload the bomb transport trailers. Modifications on the ground were therefore numerous. Some units tinkered with articulated gantries to permit handling the ordnance from the side. To ease manipulations, others went as far as installing a winch on the truck with a P.T.O., with the cable protruding through the rear floor.

But what most annoyed the users was the open cabin, and useless canvas on top which freely let in the elements. The men were reduced to customizing the

Fort Riley, Texas. An example of some clever customization: a fusion between a bomb service truck M6 and an old International Harvester K7 cargo dump 4x2. The difference in length between the two chassis affords extra room for maneuver for the man in charge of the winch. (Army SC-337625)

Above: December 2, 1944, Carolina Islands, 864th Bomb Squadron. Five companies shared the bomb-carrying trailer orders, in some cases with significant differences in their manufacturer. For instance, this trailer has a front suspension made of leaf springs installed parallel to the trailer's direction of travel. (U.S. Army Air Forces 64053 AC)

Right: New Guinea, December 9, 1942. M5 bomb trailers waiting with their cargo of cluster bombs. These trailers were very sophisticated, with electric brakes, which meant the M6 bomb service truck, just like the tractor truck had to be equipped with specific dashboard controls. (Army SC-169691)

cabin at the expense of visibility and a more compact design. Knocking together a few wooden planks secured rudimentary yet efficient protection against snow, ice, and rain. In other cases, the cabin was replaced with a full steel one taken from a Chevy or a General Motors truck. Some went as far as removing the whole technical element to install it on a closed chassis cabin that had been stripped of its rear beforehand.

Evolution

Bomb service trucks M6 followed the general evolution of the G-7000 Chevrolet series, but a 'winterization' program was initiated on April 1, 1943 and approved by May 6 for vehicles that needed to work in rough conditions.

On March 16, 1944, though its production had already been stopped, the project for transporting M6s on aircraft was born. The idea was simply to cut the chassis in half and affix bolted reinforcements to allow for reassembly. Once more a transformation kit was supplied, containing all the parts and a small dolly. It was necessary to give the M6 all the components necessary for off-road duties, as it would no longer be confined to airbases but follow aviation units on their campaigns. On June 1, 1944, for instance, it was recommended to procure the parts necessary to twin the rear axle, and provide the truck with a spare wheel.

Above: Great Britain, autumn 1943, this Chevy is towing two British bomb trolleys type C, maneuvering them under the bomb bay of a B-17F Flying Fortress. (U.S. Army Air Forces 26036 AC)

Below: Mohan Bari Airfield, Assam Province, India, December 1, 1944. A beast of burden at aerodromes, this model with transversal leaf springs is carrying parts from an International M-425 tractor and its trailer, which will be transported by air to China. (Army SC269598)

Trailers

Inseparable from this were the bomb-carrying trailers, which came in three variants. The main one was the bomb trailer M5, which was widely supplied to units equipped with the bomb service truck M6. Rarer were the M1 or M2 chemical service trailers, which were equipped with a gantry and hoist; though their use was similar—except the types of weaponry they carried—these were specific to the Chemical Warfare Service.

Several companies received orders for these trailers: Saginaw Stamping & Tools Co., American Seating Co., Electric Wheel Co., Oneida Ltd., and Trailer Company of America, amongst others. Each of these production lines had specific characteristics, like the location of the handbrake, the trunk's shape and the positioning of the leaf springs at the front. However, the main specifications remained the same: maximum traction speed 45 mph and a payload of 4,000 lb.; the M5 weighed 3,200 lb. empty, was 216 inches long, 94 inches wide, and 44 inches high.

Preparing for D-Day, June 6, 1944. Under the cover of an impressive camouflage net, a bomb trolley convoy is leaving the depot. (U.S. Army Air Forces 53249 AC)

Getting the bomb trolley under the plane was done manually. Winches installed in the plane enabled the accurate placement of the bombs in the racks. (U.S. Army Air Forces C26339 AC)

Between 1940 and 1945, the Ordnance Department received no fewer than 16,212 units.

Whilst widely spread, the bomb trailer M5 was not the only trailer used by the U.S. Army Air Forces. Supplying large fleets of bombers required very specific equipment that the Royal Air Force possessed. In an inverse Lend-Lease, Great Britain supplied several hundred Type C bomb trolleys, identical to those used for the loading of its large four-engine Avro Lancaster.

Bomb Lift Trolleys

The bomb service M6 was ultimately just a lifting gantry set up on the back of a truck. It was used to lift bombs and place them on a trailer, and then convey these to the aircraft where they would be loaded via a small lifting device. There were two different lifts for this purpose.

The bomb lift M1 was a trolley capable of taking a 2,000-lb. bomb. It was a manual traction trolley, and

Below, left: A bomb lift M22 from the 314th Service Group, Eighth Air Force, Honington, England, June 15, 1944. (U.S. Army Air Forces A72067)

Below, right: The hydraulic mechanism of the trailer made for easy and precise maneuvering under the wings. Note the two horizontal lift levers behind the front right tire, one for the front, one for the back, which meant it was possible to approach the plane's bomb attachment apparatus at exactly the right angle. (U.S. Army Air Forces 72067)

Corporal L. Turner with Sergeant H.A. Bucko loading a 500-lb. bomb in a North American P-51, using a bomb lift M1 on which an extension has been added to adapt to the aircraft's specific characteristics. (U.S. Army Air Forces A49608)

its hydraulic articulation allowed precise positioning of the bomb under the aircraft's wings, although it generally had to be installed on a booster. The Weaver Mfg. Company delivered 20,310 units to the U.S. Army between 1940 and 1945, fully referred to as a 1-ton, 3-wheel bomb lift truck, M1.

The bomb lift M22 was more of a trailer, even if it was meant to be handled manually under the bomber's hold. With a 4,000-lb. capacity, its hydraulic lift of up to 20 inches was enough to bring the bombs close to the hold's winches, which then maneuvered the bombs in. Weaver manufactured 4,037 of these 2-ton, 6-wheel bomb lift trucks, M22.

England, February 19, 1945. M22 lifts waiting to load 92nd Bombardment Group aircraft. The Luftwaffe was no longer a threat by that time, so depot camouflage was negligible. (U.S. Army Air Forces 75610)

8 Telephone Trucks

Telephone Maintenance Truck K-43

This series was complicated from an administrative point of view. These very technical trucks were equipped with a winch at the rear, or not. Orders for both versions together came to 4,229 145-inch wheelbase vehicles, with all of them delivered.

Of the 182 G-4112s and 4,047 G-7173s, Defense Aid and Lend-Lease accounted for 133 units.

Whilst the production of the 182 G-4112s amounted to a footnote in the production run, it was also the beginning of a model manufactured especially for the Signal Corps. There already existed a series of smaller vehicles for the maintenance of phone lines, but they were of the same kind as other trucks in the U.S. Army of the 1930s: small and adapted to the existing infrastructure. With the rapid rise in the number of military facilities, it was necessary to increase the capacity of the units charged with maintaining the primary communication means of the time. They had to be able to create complex networks as quickly as possible, and for this they needed vehicles that were perfectly suited to these large-scale tasks. The 1½-ton,

Type K-43 YP-G 4112-YA in working position with its lifting gear set up to erect telephone posts. The fuel tank at the back of the cabin made for a short body. (U.S. Army SC-121272)

A rare side view of one of 67 YP-G 4112-YB type K-42s. Without a winch (which would have been seen on the side of the trunk at the front), these telephone maintenance vehicles were only used for minor interventions. (U.S. Army SC-121273)

Type K-43 P-G 4112-YA in transit position. The lifting equipment prevents the driver from opening his door. The absence of a periscope in the roof denotes a pre-series model. (U.S. Army Signal Corps)

4x4 Chevrolet chassis was once more chosen as a starting point of design for the new vehicle. (We will not go into detail about the 67 YP-G 4112-YBs, or the 1,377 units of the G-7163, unknown suffix, as they only differed from the majority by the absence of the rear winch and lifting mechanism. These 1,444 vehicles were used only in the maintenance of airbase lines, whilst the others had a much wider scope, which also included the creation of these lines.)

YP-G 4112-YA Type K-43

Orders from the U.S. Army refer to 115 vehicles of this model, more commonly known as a telephone pole setter with winch. The K-43 was a semi-closed

Type K-43 YP-G 4112-YA. The rear design is clear here, apart from the vise, which has not yet been positioned. The horizontal rod is located low so as to get a direct floor-level action. (U.S. Army Signal Corps)

working machine. Its body was made up of three sides with a flexible tarpaulin and metal roof, which could be uncovered to about two-thirds. The technical ensemble was a complex system that required input from several manufacturers, like the American Coach & Body Company, or the Highway Trailer Company, which joined forces with Chevrolet.

The thick panels on the side served two purposes. On the outside, doors gave access to equipment storage and hooks could hold long objects like ladders and

Camp Adair, Oregon, August 2, 1944. A type K-43 YP-G 4112-YA from the 9th Service Command (note the insignia on the door) is reeling in cable from a special reel that has been affixed to the winch's side extension. (U.S. Army SC-304461)

August 1943. At a public display in Washington, two type K-43 YP-G 4112-YAs are installing a sign. (U.S. Army SC-240973)

A G-7173-NS K-43 with all its side doors open, and ladder and lifting gear in transport position. The body is now against the cabin and the fuel tank is no longer visible. (U.S. Army SC-380088)

poles; on the inside, long shelves and racks were for stowage of tools and the apparatus necessary to build communication lines.

An essential element of the K-43, the winch was located in the body and was controlled from the cabin via a P.T.O. linked to the transmission chain. This setup meant that the fuel tank had to relocate from its horizontal position between the longerons to the vertical behind the cabin, with its filling hole turned to the right.

The winch had multiple uses, linked to a lifting gear, the dismantled elements of which were stowed

Right side view of a type K-43 G-7173-NS. Note the lateral axis of the winch in the front trunk as well as the through-hole in the door. (U.S. Army SC-380090)

sideways on the left, blocking the driver's door; it was used for lifting heavy materials and setting up poles. It was also equipped with a lateral axis that extended all the way to the right side of the body and was fitted with a reel for the lines and cables. But it could also work autonomously, as a direct traction tool towards the back, the cable passing on the floor or higher up by the crane. This crane could be positioned at the rear sides or higher and could help unwind cable and line reels.

Other smaller accessories could be found on the K-53. Even if it was not present on the pre-series model, the driver had a periscope installed on the roof of the cabin, which could be used to position the vehicle and help activate the winch when work was taking place behind. Two telescopic legs allowed the truck to remain steady during lifting maneuvers, and for the same purpose a vise was set up at the back. There was a multitude of anchor points and a spare wheel inside the main body.

Tinian Island, Mariana Archipelago, February 1945. Full gear, accessories, and apparatus inside this G-7173-NS K-43 that belongs to the 443rd Signal Heavy Construction Battalion. (U.S. Army SC-380089)

CENSUS OF REGISTRATIONS ALLOCATED TO WINCHLESS TRUCKS TYPE K-42				
Contract	**Year**	**Body Type**	**Registration**	**Total Units**
W-398-QM-8778	1941	YP-G 4112-YB telephone maintenance	(W-002968 to W-003034)	67
W-374-ORD-018-517	1944	YP-G 4112-YB telephone maintenance	(0080014 to 0080855)	842
W-374-ORD-018-517	1944	YP-G 4112-YB telephone maintenance	(0097813 to 0098184) (0099777 to 0099939)	535

CENSUS OF REGISTRATIONS ALLOCATED TO TRUCKS TYPE K-43 WITH WINCH				
Contract	**Year**	**Body Type**	**Registration**	**Total Units**
W-398-QM-8778	1941	YP-G 4112-YA telephone pole setter w/winch	(W-002852 and (W-002854 to W-002967)	115
W-398-QM-11508	1942	G-7173-NS telephone maintenance w/winch	(007213 to 007393) (007932 to 007957) (0016555 to 0016591) (0033 to 0035613)	2,670

G-7173-NS Type K-43

After the 115 units of the G-4112, there was no further order for the G-4000 assimilated series, and only when the third series was underway did the order for 4,047 telephone maintenance G-7163-NSs materialize. There were no big structural changes between the

A 5-ton K-37 trailer, telephone construction and combination cable hauler, being towed by a K-43. This trailer with electric brakes was not usually meant to be towed by a Chevrolet, but the requirements of active service took precedence over standard operating procedure. (U.S. Army SC-380075)

A 2-ton K-36 trailer, used for telephone construction and pole hauling. The stability of the poles is ensured by four sliding vertical stands. The key was good balance and an experienced driver. (U.S. Army SC-380076)

March 16, 1945, Lungling, China. Establishing the line along the Burma Road, this G-7173-NS is loading poles. This vehicle belongs to the 432nd Signal Heavy Construction Battalion. (U.S. Army SC-218464)

Easier to use, the pole allowed for manually unwinding the cables and an easier passage on rough terrain. This trailer was favored over the K-37 when the reels were not too large. (U.S. Army SC-380106)

The 443rd Signal Heavy Construction Battalion displaying part of its fleet. From left, in front is a G-7163-NR, then two G-7173-NSs. Behind is a G-7163-NR, a G-7173-NS, then a YP-G 4112-YA. In the background is a GMC CCKW-353 compressor, a 44-C ditching machine from Barber-Greene and a D4 bulldozer. (U.S. Army SC-218464)

two productions as the vehicle retained the same function. The sides of the body were modified however, extended so as to get closer to the cabin, and therefore increase the length of some of the storage compartments and the working area inside. The fuel tank was moved to the left, at the back of the technical part and the fuel filler hole was now level with the driver's door window.

Trailers

Whichever K-53 version was used, it could be coupled with a transmission-specific trailer, of which there were two main models.

The 2-ton telephone construction and pole hauling K-36 trailers were small transport platforms with extensible tillers, manufactured by American Coach & Body Co., and Highway Trailer Co., amongst others. Their main function was to transport long objects such as telephone poles. Made of a chassis frame with a tiller and a fixed axle with 7.5x20 8-ply tires, it had a flat floor for normal transport, and four small removable drop-sides, two of them with mudguards, as accessories. One feature was four folding panels, which once in position could slide on an axis to serve as side walling for the goods being transported. This model benefited from no braking system other than its handbrake.

The 5-ton telephone construction and combination cable hauler K-37 trailers were specially designed to unwind the large phone cable reels, and to transport lengthy items. Manufactured by Highway Trailer Co., amongst others, they were made of a chassis frame with a tiller and a fixed axle with 9x20 10-ply tires. They did not have a flat floor like the K-36. One feature was two folding front panels, which once in position could slide on an axis to serve as side walling for the goods being transported, as well as two supports linked by an axis to hold wire reels. There was also an option of adding two more panels to completely enclose the goods. Equipped with an electric braking system, they were not fitted with an extensible tiller.

Telephone Earth Borer K-44

This model was inseparable from the telephone maintenance K-43 as each was reliant on the other for their purpose. 1,659 vehicles on a 145-inch wheelbase were ordered and delivered.

Of the 81 G-4112s and 1,578 G-7173s, Lend-Lease figures record 35 units sent to Allied countries.

Their very specific mission was to bore holes to fit the telephone, telegraph, and occasionally electricity poles. Known as earth borer and pole setter truck K-44 when used by the Signal Corps, it became earth auger truck M1 in the Corps of Engineers. Two types succeeded each other, one in the G-4112 series, and the other in the G-7000 assimilated series.

YP-G-4112-YC Type K-44

The first order for the 1½-ton, 4x4 Chevrolet-mounted auger was modest, only 81 vehicles. The K-44 was an

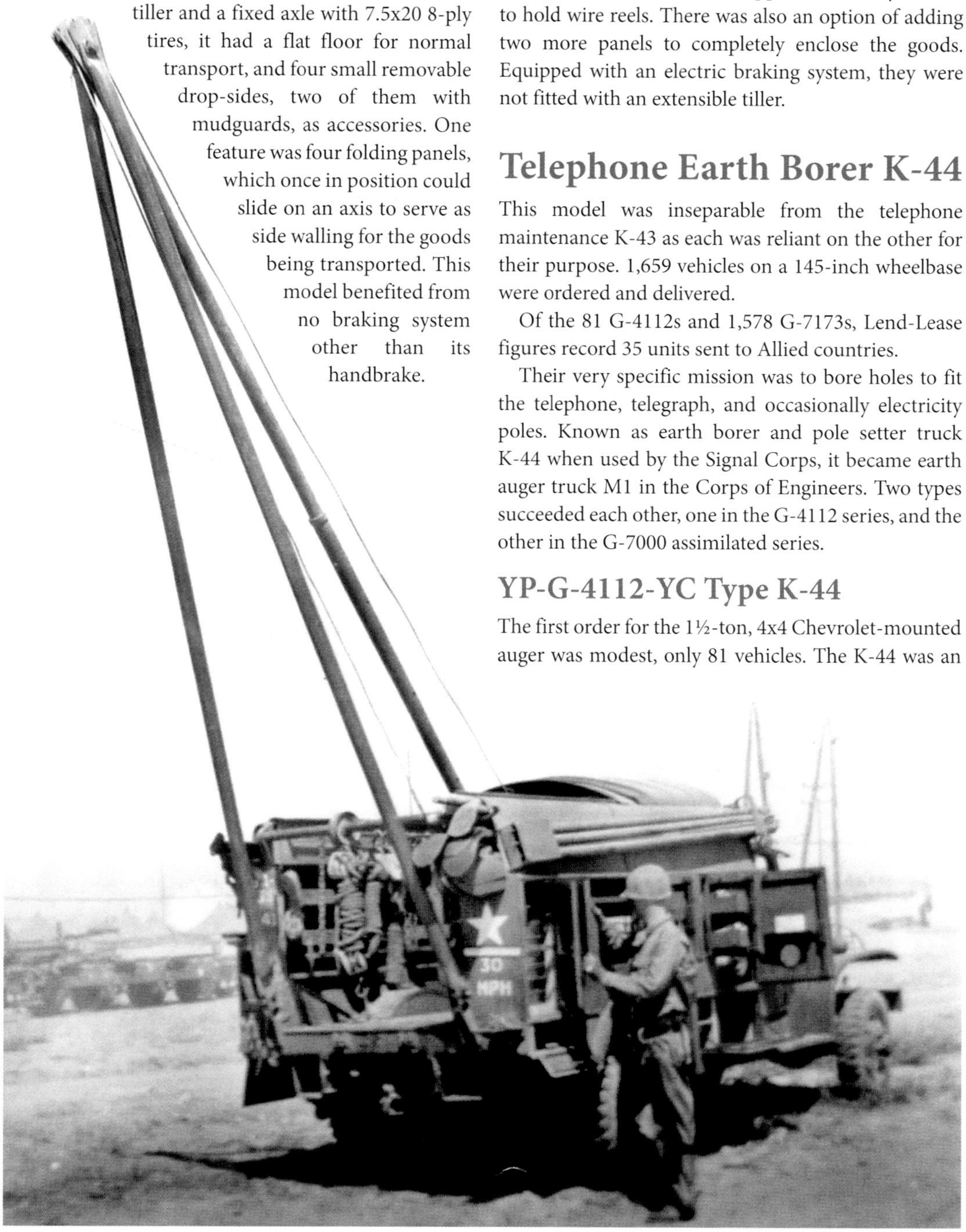

Oujda region, Morocco, June 18, 1943. This G-7173-NS from Company A, 63rd Signal Battalion, has deployed its lifting gear, the feet of which are positioned into slots at the bottom of the body. The main load strut, which can be extended to allow for slight tilt variation, is affixed to the body floor, just in front of the winch. (U.S. Army SC-185236)

This pre-series YP-G 4112-YC K-44 was photographed as it was presented to the U.S. Army. It doesn't as yet have the periscope in the roof of the cabin that allows the driver to see what's happening in the back of the vehicle. (U.S. Army Signal Corps)

A YP-G 4112-YC K-44 in work position with the auger's mast at the vertical. Note the two command levers on the left and the cable reel affixed to the winch's side axis. (U.S. Army SC-145267)

open machine, the technical elements of the body had no protection against the weather, and its sides were simple and angular. Overall manufacture was left to the same companies, now joined by the Hyatt Bearing Company. The fuel tank was fitted between the cabin and the technical part of the vehicle.

Two mechanical elements were added to the body, a multi-function winch, and an auger. The winch was connected by a P.T.O. via a transmission chain and was controlled from the cabin. Whilst it could be used in reverse, it was mostly used with the auger's mast for lifting and handling purposes. It was also equipped with a side axis that extended to the right side of the body, which was fitted with a reel to rewind lines and telephone cables. The winch supplied by the American Coach and Body Company (Type A-328 for the K-33 and A-332 for the K-44) had a 10,000-lb. force.

This extraordinary drilling machine is the perfect application of the principle of movement translation through gears and racks. Only one man is needed to operate the rig. With this model, installed on a G-4112 chassis, it was dangerous work for the operator because of stone and rubble flying all over the place. (U.S. Army Signal Corps)

Zoom in on a YP-G 4112-YCs K-44's auger. A protective box shields the winch from the weather and prevents injury. (U.S. Army Signal Corps)

A G-7163-NR K-44 seen from above with the auger in transport position, the mast resting on the edge of the body. (U.S. Army SC-380077)

The auger, manufactured by the Highway Trailer Company, was powered the same P.T.O. as the winch. The auger operator had three levers to maneuver the drilling mechanism: one to straighten the mast vertically, the other two to control the left and right rotation of the drill head. These maneuvers were made with the operator on the ground, next to the machine, which could be very dangerous. There were four different heads to choose from depending on the task required, each with a specific drilling diameter of 9, 12, 16, or 20 inches.

Above, left: Near Shadazup on the Ledo Road between India and China, the 96th Signal Construction Battalion is establishing a phone line. Col. George F. Moynahan, S/Sgt Wilbur T. Hansen and Pfc Fred B. Walker follow the progress of the auger being handled by T4 Alfred N. Pizzio. (U.S. Army SC-274291)

Above, right: August 1944, the 508th Port Battalion unloading Liberty Ship *Henry T. Scott* at the King George Docks, Calcutta, India. A Chevrolet G-7163-NR is exiting the ship's hold. Note the two different auger heads on the left, the container at the rear being used to store the smaller ones. (U.S. Army SC-194903)

Hirschtal, Germany, December 1944. The 120th Engineer Combat Battalion of the 45th Infantry Division has asked for the help of an auger Chevy from the 57th Signal Construction Battalion, Sixth Army Group, to drill a road and mine it more easily. (U.S. Army Signal Corps)

Holabird Signal Depot, Baltimore, Maryland, February 13, 1945. Amidst GMC CCKW-353 K-60s and Chevrolet G-7173-NS K-43s, K-44s await transfer. Note the extensible stabilizers installed under the body. (U.S. Army P-13-2-45-710)

CENSUS OF REGISTRATIONS ALLOCATED TO AUGER TRUCKS K-44 WITH WINCH

Contract	Year	Body Type	Registration	Total Units
W-398-QM-8778	1941	YP-G 4112-YC telephone earth borer w/winch	(W-002853 and W-003035 to W-003114)	81
W-398-QM-11508	1942	G-7163-NR telephone earth borer w/winch	(007394 to 007518) (007958 to 007986) (0016592 to 0016794) (0032262 to 0032580)	676
W-374-ORD-018-517	1944	G-7163-NR telephone auger borer & pole setter	(0080856 to 0081142)	287
W-374-ORD-018-517	1944	G-7163-NR Telephone earth borer w/winch	(0092362 to 0092473) (0098957 to 0099094) (0099305 to 0099669)	615

The Dorff region in Germany, 2nd Signal Construction Battalion, Ninth Army. The operator's position on this G-7163-NR is very different from that of the YP-G 4112-YC. He is now able to handle it without fear of getting tangled in the machine. (U.S. Army SC-190810)

G-7163-NR Type K-44

This model was characterized by significant overall changes. The structure of the technical body was completely redesigned, with the sharp angles at the rear giving way to softer curves. It was lengthened to be nearer to the cabin, which meant the fuel tank had to be moved to the left at the bottom of the technical body. A new auger model was installed, and operation was now done from within the truck. The side trunks were enlarged, and the opening now had two sliding panels rather than one.

The Signal Corps' vehicles were varied and should not be confused. Thus, the K-43 and K-44 were specially dedicated to the Signal Construction Battalion, whether Light, Normal or Heavy. These general reserve units were mostly attached to armies or army groups. A Signal Construction Battalion was comprised of two companies, each with two sections. The battalion was allocated eight K-36 trailers, 16 K-43 and eight K-44 trucks. A Signal Heavy Construction Battalion was allocated twice this: 16 K-36 trailers, 32 K-43, and 16 K-44 trucks.

September 1948, Seoul, Korea. This G-7163-NR from the 66th Signal Construction Battalion is being used to repair the phone line with an aerial bucket. The lift is carried out by the winch cable, which acts via the pulley located at the top of the auger's mast. As it is impossible to always ensure a flat parking area for the truck, the auger has to compensate for both axes: left to right and front and back. (U.S. Army Signal Corps)

9 Chassis Cab Trucks

A specific category in the 1½-ton, 4x4 Chevrolet line, the chassis cab had four main uses.

The first is unclear, as it had no specific task, and it is difficult to find mention of it in any records; the second and third were turret trainer and field lighting trucks allocated to the U.S. Army Air Forces. The fourth category was fire trucks that were specifically destined for the Corps of Engineers.

Like most U.S. Army suppliers, Chevrolet delivered vehicles with bare chassis, with nothing at the rear.

These vehicles consisted of the chassis, complete with mechanical components and an equipped cabin (though the field lighting trucks had an added empty platform). There was no electrical braking system for a potential trailer, not even a spare wheel hatch (apart from the J-3 and J-4), this latter being temporarily placed in the cabin; it was up to the company which had received the order to offer a technical solution, or the military users to find a suitable place for it.

Of the 217 G-4112-YPs, 142 G-7143-NFs, and 6,748 G-7103-NEs, the fire trucks, the turret trainer E-5s, and the field lighting trucks were the best-known models. All 7,107

The chassis cab Chevrolets were stripped to a minimum, without even a spare wheel bracket: the spare wheel was delivered in the cab. (SNL G-85 Vol. IV)

It was difficult to tell the difference between a bare chassis and a tractor truck without seeing the registration number. (U.S. army SC-123888)

vehicles had a 145-inch wheelbase. Some 4,112 units were ordered under the contract reference W-374-ORD-20-18-517 (1944) or with technical bodies of all types. Twenty were sent to Russia as part of Lend-Lease and 1,466 units switched roles: 104 were converted to winchless cargo dump trucks and 1,362 to straightforward winchless cargo trucks.

Only 2,646 units were submitted to non-standard customization. The Corps of Engineers found the compact size of the truck advantageous during operations in the jungles of the Pacific islands, and fitted compressors, pumps and all sorts of technical equipment onto it. These bare chassis were also the subject of a series of tests for the creation of medium-sized wreckers, though nothing came of it. Towards the end of the war, others were upgraded as fire trucks to add to those which had already been ordered.

Turret Trainer Truck E-5

According to the U.S. Army Air Forces TM 9-2800 technical manual, these vehicles were developed for aircraft gunnery students to practice shooting live ammunition from the different types of turrets in use.

Above: New Guinea, October 22, 1943, a turret trainer truck E5 in its most basic form. The turret support is very basic and the mechanisms simplified as far as possible. The generator is dangerously exposed here. (ACME A-801-38)

Right: Replenishing ammunition in the same vehicle. To prevent serious accidents, belts were kept short with a maximum of 60 bullets. (ACME A-801-39)

The Panama Canal. S/Sgt Arthur H. Gentleman is instructing Sgt Felix A. Beauregard. The structure of the fixed training turret was higher than that used during mobile exercises. (U.S. Army Air Forces B-49373)

Space was at a premium on the truck. When fire was taken from behind, the small running board was inadequate and the instructors were obliged to stand on the roof of the cab. (ACME A-685-47)

Above, left: August 1943, Gunnery School at Laredo Army Airfield, Texas. At this stage of training, the turret cannot rotate farther than the blocking lateral rods, one of which is visible in the foreground. (U.S. Army Air Forces 238-259)

Above, right: August 10, 1942, Gunnery School at Harlingen, Texas. Having mastered the equipment with horizontal shooting on both fixed and mobile targets, students moved on to shooting from any angle. Balloons were used as enemy planes and tracer bullets were used to adjust the fall of shot. (AP Wirephoto LD-21100)

This side view of the turret trainer truck E5, registered 6044616, gives us a good idea of the overall layout. Note the support points for the stabilizers near the front bumper and in front of the twin wheels at the rear. After their instruction on an open turret, students were taught to deal with the confined space found in bombers. (Private collection)

Right: The ventral Sperry turret also had its own adapted gantry on this turret trainer truck E5. More complex than normal, the structure was made with a large cantilever beam which was maintained by four suspension struts. (Private collection)

These used fixed ground or mobile air targets, from either a fixed or moving platform to simulate flying conditions.

Just like its predecessors, delivered with a bare chassis, their reference was G-7103-NE, apart from the first two models which were G-4113-ZPs, model ZK, W-607641, and W-607642. Some 1,620 units were ordered for the U.S. Army, a number of which evolved into the field lighting truck J-5. Contract W-398-QM-12945 (1942) dealt with 199 trucks, registration numbers 6044503 to 6044701, and contract W-398-QM-11510 (1942) with two orders, one of 1,108 vehicles (6061126 to 6062233), the second of 313 units (6092653 to 6092965).

The turret trainer truck E-5 was the result of a collaboration with the Herman Body Company, St Louis, Missouri. The company took care of the frame which was fixed to the chassis, as well as a large storage trunk, on top of which the spare wheel was fitted. Two stabilization points were installed in front of the rear wheels, and at the front of the chassis two further stabilization points were installed. The aim was to ensure the stability of the vehicle and provide extra support during lengthy shooting sessions. As all bomber turrets were controlled electrically, a generator was placed in the storage trunk, where the spare wheel would be on a standard Chevrolet. It was linked to a P.T.O. installed with the mechanical components.

Another configuration with the front and rear turrets of the B-24 Liberator. Tarpaulins were placed under the machine guns to catch the spent cartridges. (Private collection)

A frame of steel beams was set up on the base, which was topped by a rudimentary turret for preliminary training. It was simply made of a rotation mechanism, a cradle composed of a seat and two 12.7-mm machine guns, and without glass to allow the instructor direct contact with the student. For advance training, the turret trainer E-5 was fitted with the main turret models: dorsal, ventral, or nose for the B-17, B-25, and B-24, for example.

Field Lighting Trucks

Field lighting trucks were also specific to the U.S. Army Air Forces. They were conceived at the Wright-Patterson Air Force Base in Dayton, Ohio in 1941.

The primary aim of these trucks was to create coded light signals for nocturnal takeoffs and landings on improvised or captured enemy airfields. Secondly, their projectors' power meant they could also be used to light up work areas or crash zones. They were referred to as J-3, J-4, and J-5.

At first, all three models of these strange vehicles, also built on a 145-inch wheelbase, were ordered together, totaling 313 units. They were known as G-7143-NF chassis field lighting trucks. In 1942, 100 units were delivered to an unregistered country as part of the Defense Aid program (contract reference DA-W-535-AC-888); 142 more of them were produced under contract W-535-AC-19340 (numbered 609058 to 609199). The 71 J-3/J-4s remaining were manufactured in 1943 under contract 95055 with the U.S. Navy. The exact number of J-5s is unknown, as they were lost amongst the chassis cab order of contract W-398-QM-11510, which concerned G-7103-NEs registered 6061126 to 6062233.

Mobile Floodlights Illuminate Emergency Landing Fields

PORTABLE floodlights, mounted on powerful, four-wheel-drive trucks, and equipped with hoods that prevent enemy flyers from seeing them, have been designed at Wright Field, Dayton, Ohio, for illuminating emergency fields for night take-offs and landings. Each truck carries six floodlights.

Power plant and floodlights on truck, above, provide eyes for night flyers. Right, covered over for dash to field

Above: In this article from the 1941 magazine *Popular Science*, a field lighting truck J-3 displays two of its particularities: the deployment of its lighting tower and its tarpaulin protection. The base for the vehicle being a G-4112, it is probably a prototype of the series.

Field Lighting Trucks J-3 and J-4

The two versions, which only differed by the power generator they used, were the result of the collaboration between Chevrolet—that supplied the chassis with a

The first version of the field lighting truck J-3, with no other equipment than the two small storage trunks at the rear. (SNL G-85 Vol. IV)

A field lighting truck J-4 with its lighting ramps in low position. The difference between this model's body and the previous one is obvious. (Private collection)

Instruction on a field lighting truck J-4. It was important for the runway crew to know how to handle all the equipment at their disposal. (U.S. Army Signal Corps)

platform under which the spare wheel was fixed—and the American Gas Accumulator Company in Elizabeth, New Jersey. The latter specialized in maritime signaling, its main products being illuminating buoys and beacons. The company was famed for its work lighting up the Panama Canal, but it was its mastery of large-scale lenses that granted it access to this military project. The J-3 and J-4 supported three ramps of two projectors, the whole thing being mounted on a manually controlled telescopic post. The technical platform was made of wood and had three drop-sides with tailgate, which created an access footboard. Apart from the group's characteristics, the J-3 could be recognized by the two small handrails installed on the sides' last tier and its two small storage trunks, whilst the J-4's handrails occupied the entire side and only had one trunk. Both required a 110-volt power supply.

Right: San Francisco, December 23, 1941. The cleaning of the lenses was absolutely critical as without regular maintenance the efficiency of the six projectors was largely diminished with invasive shadows impairing visibility. (ACME 19430)

Below: According to the registration number, this field lighting truck is a fire truck hybrid. On display in Wilmington, North Carolina, we can see the back of the projectors.

Right: The same vehicle seen from the back. The G.I. on the working platform gives us an idea of the height of the apparatus and the size of the lenses. (Private collection)

Below: Field lighting truck J-5 in operational mode with the projectors at full height. Note that the storage trunk is not as yet installed on this model. (Private collection)

Field Lighting Truck J-5

This version had fewer projectors and was manufactured by the Davey Compressor Company in Somerset, Pennsylvania. It differed from the others in its use of a generator that was powered by the mechanical components of the truck itself and linked to it by a chain. On the J-5, the four projectors were positioned two by two in a square. They were mounted on a telescopic mast which supported a bracket on each side, onto which the spotlights could rotate. Whilst it still retained storage space in the trunk, accessible by the tailgate that doubled as a footboard, this version had a simplified body structure, which meant easier access to the technical elements. Contrary to the previous models, J-5s were supplied with a bare chassis. It should also be noted that the technology used, together with the specific electric materials, only allowed for a 32-volt power supply.

In order to fit two extra trunks and increase the storage space, the spare wheel relocated from the left longeron

to the technical base. Thanks to its round projectors, the field lighting J-5 truck offered better lighting and was valued by the cinematographic units of the Signal Corps, who, as soon as they could, turned these vehicles into mobile projectors for their outdoor sets.

Fire Trucks

Typical American vehicles, the fire trucks were specifically destined for the Engineer Fire Fighting Detachments (E.F.F.D.s) from the Corps of Engineers. The first ten units were designed in August 1942, at Camp Clairborne, Louisiana.

Originally composed of volunteers from various Army units, they became the backbone of the first firefighting units. Before that, the role of firefighter was a civilian domain. These E.F.F.D.s were numbered from 1 to 10, and apart from two which were sent directly to England, the others spent their service, from April 1, 1943, in North Africa. In August of the same year, these units were renamed Engineer Fire Fighting Platoons (E.F.F.P.s) with new numbering from 1201 to 1210. They were specially assigned to the U.S. Army. At the same time, Engineer Aviation Fire Fighting Platoons (E.A.F.F.P.s) were created, their mission being to protect airbases. In time, the number of these firefighting units rose proportionately with the Army's, but intervening in civilian fires was never a consideration: the infrastructures of the countries being liberated (or conquered) were meant to be sufficient to cope with civilian needs. It was also at that time that the E.F.F.P. changed its name and became the Engineer Composite Section (E.C.S.).

Up until December 7, 1941 the majority of the fire trucks operating on U.S. bases were painted regulatory red, and it was only after the disaster of Pearl Harbor and the impressive destruction of firefighting equipment, that they started being painted Olive Drab. Towards the end of the war, however, as the E.F.F.P and E.A.F.F.P. became part of the armies of occupation, old habits prevailed, and the military fire trucks regained their bright red coats. From 1941 to 1943, 1,201 fire trucks were ordered from Chevrolet, mention being made of both their uniqueness and their pumping power. These fire trucks were the result of the collaboration between three manufacturers: the vehicle's, the company that

August 1944 somewhere in France, an Engineer firefighting platoon on exercise. Although it was not strictly its role, this Class 325 fire truck or brush truck 325 is being used for training in a civilian intervention. (Associated Press 10950C)

Above: Liège, Belgium, November 28, 1944, the 12th Engineer Fire Fighting Platoon departs its cantonment. This unit spent several weeks in the city of Mosane, stationed there to help the local populace during the V-1 bombings that took place in the area. (U.S. Army SC-197238)

Below: September 12, 1944, Molesworth, England. The Class 110 did not remain in the United States, with most crossing to England. USA-501414 is seen here at the scene of a forced landing by a Flying Fortress of the 303rd Bombardment Group. (U.S. Army Air Forces 61860-A.C.)

installed the technical firefighting elements, and a pump manufacturer, the last two sometimes being one and the same. These Chevys had five classifications: classes 110, 135, 300, 325, and 525.

Crash Truck Class 110

The first 185 Class 110s made in 1941, were actually an order from the Quartermaster Corps. As the base vehicle was purchased unfinished and without a specific destination, these trucks were not referred to as Chevrolet, but a creation specific to the U.S. Army. They were identified by a plate affixed to each side of the engine compartment, on which read "Model 110 QMC." These trucks were equipped with a Hale-H pump for the first 30 (W-501702 to W-50731) or an American LaFrance for the other 155 (W-501274 to W-501428). These 185 vehicles, originally referred to as Airfield Service, were built on G-4112-YP-type Chevrolets. Some 191 new crash trucks Class 110 on G-7103-NE chassis made up the numbers in an order dated 1942. They were all fitted with an American LaFrance pump. Some 151 of them were assembled by the Engineering Depot (W-50376 to W-503918, plus W-503920), whilst the other 40 were assembled by Oren Fire Apparatus (W-503961 to 504000).

Crash trucks were, as their name suggests, specifically designed to fight fires created by airplane crashes. They were of modest size, but perfectly adapted to dealing with accidents involving fighter aircraft. They were equipped with a centrifugal pump that was mounted in the center of the chassis and which had a 100-gpm flow rate, working with a pressure of 7 bars. Connected to a 100-foot-long, 1½-inch-diameter hose, the pump was fed by a 250-gallon tank of water mixed with a

The first model of a crash truck Class 110 on a G-4112-YP chassis. The 185 units of this series were assembled by the Quartermaster Corps. (U.S. Army Signal Corps)

foaming agent. The vehicle was also equipped with a 300-lb. CO_2 gas installation, which was connected to a 100-foot-long, ½-inch-diameter hose on a reel. At full capacity, these vehicles had an operational period of 2½ minutes, which was more than enough to put out a fire on a monospar aircraft..

Crash Truck Class 135

Some 425 crash trucks were ordered in 1942, with a pump manufactured by Darley and Co., and on G-7103-NE chassis. Altogether 50 were assembled at Darley and Co. (W-506089 to W-506138), 250 at Mack Manufacturing Co. (W-506239 to W-506338, W-507843 to W-507527 and W-507578 to W-507602), and 50 more at Central Fire Truck (W-507528 to W-507577). In 1943, two new purchase orders were placed, one for 100 vehicles from Oren Fire Apparatus (508332 to 508431), and the other for 60 machines from American LaFrance (5010029 to 5010088), which came to a total of 585 fire trucks Class 135, on 1½-ton, 4x4 Chevrolet chassis.

Particular to these trucks was the high-pressure (35 bars) pump, with a 100-gpm flow rate, on an extended chassis in front of the radiator grille. They were equipped with a 300-gallon cistern and a 20-gallon equivalent reserve of powdered foaming agent. There were three reels installed low on the truck, each with a 150-foot-long, ¾-inch-diameter hose. These vehicles had a maximum operational period of 3 minutes.

This crash truck Class 135, registration number 506113, was assembled at Darley and Co. with a pump from the same manufacturer. The rear view shows the low positioning of the three reels. (U.S. Army Signal Corps)

Brush truck Class 300 assembled by Darley and Co. with a front pump from American Marsh. (U.S. Army Signal Corps)

Apart from the two mounted reels, the Class 300's overall design and large mudguards were reminiscent of the first Class 110. (U.S. Army Signal Corps)

Brush truck Class 325 with a Darley and Co. pump, assembled and equipped by the Maxim Company. (U.S. Army Signal Corps)

Because of their function, the brush truck Class 325 received a multitude of accessories: sprayer, bucket, and other tools to put out bushfires. (U.S. Army Signal Corps)

Occupied Germany, 1949. In the Heidelberg military Fire Station No. 1, an Engineer Composite Section (E.C.S.) shows off its fire trucks: two Class 525 Chevrolets flank a Dodge WC-51. (U.S. Army SC-317491)

Somewhere on the road to India, a Chevy crash truck Class 135 on standby at a U.S. Army Air Forces aerodrome. (U.S. Army Air Forces 72343-A.C.)

July 29, 1944, a similar scene in England. A Class 135 from the 2095th Engineer Aviation Fire Fighting Platoon (401st Bombardment Group, Eighth U.S.A.A.F) on standby with a Fordson WOT1 fire crash tender. (U.S. Army Air Forces 72343-A.C.)

Ordnance Depot, Lima, Ohio. A group photo at the end of a team's service. This modified Chevrolet brush truck Class 300 is flanked by an American LaFrance fire truck Class 750 and a fire truck Class 500 on a Ford chassis with Cayasler equipment. (U.S. Army Signal Corps)

Brush Truck Class 300

Another category, the brush truck, was conceived for use within army bases and camps. Their main task was to deal with forest and bush fires. In 1943, 75 vehicles were ordered from Darley and Co. with a 300-gpm American Marsh pump placed at the front. Equipped with a 250-gallon cistern, they were easily recognizable thanks to their two reels installed above the technical elements, both fitted with a 150-foot-long, 1-inch-diameter hose. To allow for prolonged interventions, it was possible to connect the vehicle to a water distribution network via hydrants. For this purpose, a 1,000-foot-long flexible hose was positioned above the cistern, and, if necessary, connecting hoses could also be used.

Brush Truck Class 325

Similar to the Class 300, the Class 325 was specially designed for use abroad. It simply possessed a larger, 300-gallon cistern, and the two hose reels were installed low on each side of the truck body. In 1943, 125 units were ordered, fitted with a Darley and Co. pump and with Maxim equipment.

Fire Truck Class 525

These were hybrid trucks, ordered in a rush in 1943. Class 525 fire trucks were traditional fire engine trucks, especially designed to fight building fires. Equipped with a Darley and Co. 500-gpm frontal pump, they were meant to act as a relay between the water distribution point and its hoses; the 150-gallon tank was there only to ensure the proper priming of the hose. They had a rigid 150-foot, 1-inch diameter hose reel at the back, but their main asset was a 1,000-foot, 2½-inch flexible hose with which to connect to the water mains, and which could also be used as a high-pressure hose. Only 40 units of this type were ordered in 1943 on a G-7103-NE chassis; the equipment manufacturer was Oren Fire Apparatus.

Saipan Island, Mariana Archipelago, June 23, 1944, a typical large airfield in the Pacific. From left are a Chevrolet crash truck Class 135, an intervention Jeep, and a WC-54 Dodge ambulance. (U.S. Army Air Forces A63670-A.C.)

1941, military exercises in North Carolina with the 65th Observation Group. This crash truck Class 100 recently in-service carries registration number W-50731, indicating that it is the 30th and last vehicle of the first series. It is shiny new in its Olive Drab paint with chromed searchlight on the cabin and siren on the left wing. (Private collection)

Lido di Camaiore, Italy. A posed photograph of a Chevy from the 1206th Engineer Composite Section, Fifth U.S. Army. The classic red of the fire trucks reappeared at the end of the war. (U.S. Army Signal Corps C-587)

After 1943, there were no further orders of Chevrolet 4x4 firefighters. Military developments, mostly concerning bombers' dimensions, and the increase in size of installations, meant that this type of vehicle became too small. Progressively, the 6x6 chassis, in different weight categories, came to replace them.

Registration number USA-507572 pertains to this crash truck Class 135 assembled by the Central Fire Truck Co., and belonging to the 521st Engineers Fire Fighting Company. (Private Collection)

10 Cab Over Engine Trucks

A total of 701 1½-ton, 4x4 Chevrolet stake & platform trucks with forward cabin were manufactured, built on a 175-inch wheelbase.

Despite representing barely 0.5 percent of the production run, these vehicles occupied a very specific niche. In all, 96 of them were G-4103s, 103 were G-7153s and 502 G-7123s; none was sent abroad as part of Defense Aid or Lend-Lease.

It might seem curious to adopt a whole new configuration, so different from the rest of the military production run, for such a small number of vehicles, but this can be explained by the need to have a larger loading surface in the technical components. This solution was identical to the one adopted by General Motors to transform its CCKW-353 into an AFKWX-353. The stake & platform offered a high cargo body, but also a free loading platform thanks to the all-round drop-sides. The Signal Corps and the Navy were the main users of these trucks, which came in three distinct configurations.

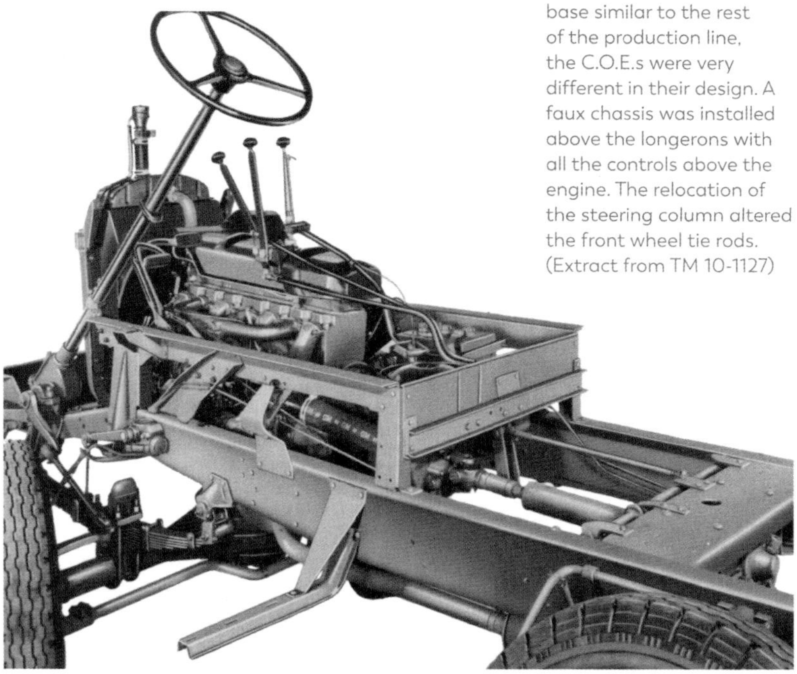

Despite a mechanical base similar to the rest of the production line, the C.O.E.s were very different in their design. A faux chassis was installed above the longerons with all the controls above the engine. The relocation of the steering column altered the front wheel tie rods. (Extract from TM 10-1127)

Below: A fine example of a Chevrolet C.O.E. G-4103 with radar antenna, it is a K-33 model in a transmission unit. Replicated from civilian lines, these vehicles were militarized, with, for example, a protective grille over the radiator. (U.S. Army Signal Corps)

Above: One of the 103 units of the G-7153-NX delivered to the U.S. Navy. The location of the tow hooks at the front under the bumper, and the absence of blackout lights, were some of the differences from those delivered to the U.S. Army. (U.S. Navy)

CENSUS OF REGISTRATIONS ALLOCATED TO CAB OVER ENGINE TRUCKS				
Contract	Year	Body Type	Registration	Total Units
W-398-QM-8686	1941	YX-G 4103-YN stake & platform with forward cabin	(W-328665 to W-328760)	96
W-398-QM-1078	1942	G 7123-NN	(343779 to 343838)	60
W-398-QM-11510	1942	G 7123-NN	(3114446 to 3114802) (3219414 to 3219498)	442
Navy-95055	1942	G 7153-NX	No registration number	103

In total, 103 were ordered by the Navy, under contract Navy-95055. These were delivered with bare chassis, reference G-7153-NX. They were then equipped by the buyer's services to be used in naval air stations as crash trucks. They were equipped with a centrifugal pump in the middle of the chassis, which had a 100-gpm flow rate, with 7 bar pressure. It was connected to a 100-foot-long, 1½-inch-diameter hose fed from a 300-gallon cistern, and with a supply of powdered foaming agent (enough to make 24 gallons). The vehicle was also equipped with a 300-lb. CO_2 reserve, also connected to a 100-foot, ½-inch hose.

In total, 598 other C.O.E.s (cab over engine trucks)—G-4106s and G-7123s, proportions unknown—were divided between short and long bodyworks. The short version was 16 feet long and the long version was 19½ feet long, more than 3 feet longer, which overhung at the back without any modification to the body. In the Signal Corps, the short models were referred to as K-33 and the long ones as K-54. They were used for the transport of the first large mobile radar panels.

Left: Brooklyn Army Base, August 1941. Wedged between two Autocar U-5044 K-32s, this C.O.E. Chevy is loaded with antenna panels for SCR-270 radars; the mast lies on one of the K-22 trailers next to it. (U.S. Army SC-124577)

Above: A convoy transporting an SCR-270 radar. From right, a GMC AFKX-804 K-31 van, a GMC AFKX-804 K-30 van, an autocar U-5044-T K-32 tractor and K-2 Couse trailer, and a Chevrolet YQ-G-4103-YN K-33. (U.S. Army Signal Corps)

Below: Side view of a Chevrolet YQ-G-4103-YN K-33, Signal Corps Laboratories, Fort Monmouth. The S&P configuration afforded the vehicle many possibilities: its individually removable drop-sides meant the loading platform could be customized. This line of vehicle quickly disappeared from the Army catalogue though, with the more conventional vehicles being able to fulfill the G-4103's various task. (U.S. Army SC-124700/701)

Above: December 21, 1942, Signal Laboratory, Camp Evans. A three-quarter view of a rare K-54 with long cargo frame. This configuration was achieved without modifying the chassis. (U.S. Army SC-193354)

Right: In the foreground is a GMC AFKX-804; on the left is a Chevrolet cab over engine K-33 waiting under an SCR-271 tower, the fixed version of the SCR-270 radar. These were the first early-warning radars, and although imprecise in 3D, they had the great advantage of having a 150-mile range depending on the altitude of the aircraft. They were also known as the Pearl Harbor Radar, as it was an SCR-270 that detected the Japanese aircraft on December 7, 1941, half an hour before they arrived at the naval base. (U.S. Army Signal Corps)

11 Lowboys

By 1941, the Army's motorization program was progressing fast, and all the large manufacturers were participating in the renewal and expansion of the vehicle fleet.

The focus was on mobility and all-wheel drive, and almost nothing was done to assist with camouflage and concealment. Apart from the Jeep, all the vehicles were high clearance and/or had wide and impressive metal cabins, most of them replicated from civilian lines.

On May 26, 1941, after examining two Ford 1½-ton, 4x4 T-5 prototypes, which left a big impression on him, the Chief of Field Artillery requested that some thought be put to the creation of low vehicles that could, amongst other things, be used as gun motor carriages. They were to have a good weight/power

Left: The front of the vehicle displays a compact grille, headlights extending no farther than the mudguards and a perfectly integrated winch. (U.S. Army ORD-785-1)

Below: A G-7129 Chevrolet, at Holabird Ordnance Base, Baltimore, Maryland, January 4, 1943. The Ordnance Department classified lowboys in relation to the driver's seat location. Here it's a driver on left-side running board to signify that the driver's position is outside the chassis. (U.S. Army ORD-785-2)

ratio, and a short wheelbase. His wish was to see the research covering all the ½-ton, 1½-ton, and 2½-ton lines. On June 27, 1941 the Quartermaster Corps Technical Committee authorized a feasibility survey for the ¾-ton, 1½-ton, and 3-ton lines. The original idea had expanded; it was no longer focused on Field Artillery vehicles only.

After consulting the main manufacturers, the Quartermaster Corps, on February 9, 1942, authorized the special purchase of 75 prototypes for 25 different models, to be realized by eight companies (Dodge, Ford, GMC, International, Studebaker, Reo, Corbitt, and Chevrolet). In order to complete the survey and

Above: A large storage trunk and a battery well were positioned side by side on the right longeron, with two spare wheels between the seats. (U.S. Army ORD-785-5)

Left: On the left side of the vehicle was the long fuel tank. The exhaust outlet is located just behind the mud flap. (U.S. Army ORD-785-6)

Below left: The rear is typically Chevrolet with the triangular edge protectors. Note also the folding seats integrated into the drop-sides. (U.S. Army ORD-785-4)

Below right: February 1943, this photograph was taken in the snow and the cab is now covered. The three-part windshield is characteristic; each panel is independent, but the two outer ones are necessary to put the cabin's canvas on. As the vacuum-operated windshield wipers are operated individually, they have different positions at rest. (U.S. Army ORD-785-10)

From the back there is little to differentiate this lowboy tactical vehicle from a traditional cargo. In direct competition with the Dodge WC-62/63, fundamentally the G-7129 did not offer anything new. Its lack of mechanical standardization with existing series was its downfall and it did not progress further than prototype stage. (U.S. Army ORD-785-11)

compare with recently purchased equipment, the Corps also ordered two ¾-ton and four 1½-ton Dodges. The comparison was made on 81 vehicles of 27 different types.

Most lowboys were of unconventional design. The driver's seat was often placed next to the engine or outside the chassis; one model had its engine placed laterally and another had its engine at the rear. The lowboy line had just come into existence and with the number of potential users having already grown, tests took place at the Aberdeen Proving Ground, Ordnance Depot of Fort Holabird in Maryland for the Quartermaster Corps, at Fort Knox, Kentucky, for the Armored Force Board, and at Fort Benning, Georgia, for the Infantry Board.

Despite encouraging results and successful tests for the majority of the vehicles, the lowboys were not series-produced, and the program was officially stopped on November 19, 1943. These low vehicles did not make enough of a difference compared to standard vehicles and the U.S. Army decided to avoid modifying the assembly lines, which would have incurred extra expenses and delays.

However, the survey had some consequences, as although shortages of metal were often used as a reason for the introduction of open cabins, it was mostly a gain of volume during transport and the overall reduction of the silhouette that was at the base of these modifications.

Chevrolet had participated in this large survey and supplied two 1½-ton vehicles, G-7129s: 3114161 and 3114152. They were a success compared to their standard line. The driver's seat outside the chassis frame enabled the reduction of the overall vehicle height. By enlarging the driving area, it was possible to fit two spare wheels, flat, between the driver's and the co-driver's seats. The windshield came in three parts; the middle was made of canvas that allowed for the transport of long objects. The mechanical elements were installed on a 137-inch wheelbase and boasted a 269-in^3 G.M.C. motor, up to 89 hp at 3,000 rpm, of a five-gear-plus-reverse Clark 2½-VO gearbox, of a two-gear Chevrolet transfer case, and Banjo-type axles.

Above, left: An alternative view of the G-7129, registration number USA-3114162. Another problem was the awkward access to the driving seat and the difficulty the crew had in getting out of the vehicle. (U.S. Army ORD-785-9)

Left: One distinctive feature was that the canvas cabin roof was pulled on with no fastening to the cargo frame, which meant that the canvas could be put on at the front to protect the driver without having to cover the rear, as only the front arch was necessary. (U.S. Army ORD-785-8)

12 The 1-ton Trailer

In the overall concept of the American fleet, trailers were indispensable accessories that increased the capacity of a vehicle. In the case of the 1½-ton, 4x4 Chevrolet, the 1-ton, 2-wheel cargo trailer was its assigned partner.

The truck and the trailer were both equipped with the same tires. It was in 1939 that this trailer made its debut in the inventory tables. The early models were manufactured by Lavine-Gear and the first 2,692 units delivered during the 1940. They did not have a lighting system, had a fixed tiller and the handbrake system was located at the front right of the chassis. It was only in early 1941 that the first large order was placed with Nash-Kelvinator for the initial 20,000 units. This

Right: November 13, 1941, Camp Robinson, Arkansas. On the early models, there was a jockey wheel with tire and inner tube. This 1-ton trailer belongs to the 43rd Engineers. (U.S. Army SC-133764)

Below: The use of the same tires on the tractor and the trailer was important for stability and allowed for perfect horizontal alignment. (U.S. Army Signal Corps)

production line had to be equipped with 7.5x20 tires, like those on the vehicles that were destined to tow them, the CCKW and the 1½-ton Chevrolet. This meant that the vehicle's spare wheel could also be used on the trailer.

Up until 1945, no fewer than 337,829 trailers of this type were ordered from around 30 companies. The main six were Ben Hur (66,053 units), Gerstenlager (61,365 units), Checker Cab (53,845 units), Nash-Kelvinator (44,628 units), American Bantam (27,000 units), and Willys Overland (18,000 units); the other 24 manufacturers received orders ranging from six to 6,989 units.

In 1944, with the rapid advance of American forces in all theaters, the Ordnance Department revised its needs and cut 78,765 trailers from their order books, officially only producing, according to the Report of Acceptance, 259,064 1-ton, 2-wheel cargo trailers. This might seem strange, but it had been anticipated in the Army's contract clauses. This latter gave preference to a vast reconditioning program of the existing material, which in this instance concerned 38,833 1-ton trailers, 7,658 of them revamped in 1944, and 31,175 in 1945. Curiously, considering the large number of trailers produced, few (only 18,949 units) were sent as part of Defense Aid and Lend-Lease. France received 10,875 units, China 4,376, Britain 2,704 and a multitude of smaller quantities went to others.

Three Main Lines

Total production included three main lines: models 41-33 and 41-120 from Ben Hur amounted to 49,956 units, 111,465 units of Model A were manufactured by Gerstenlager and Nash-Kalvinator, and 74,562 units of the T-6 model were built by 13 of the 30 manufacturers.

The first 1-tonners made in 1940 were built without a wheel on the parking stand; a simple stand like the one on the Jeep's trailer was installed, but here the similarities stopped. Several differences were in evidence. Without necessarily being able to attribute these details to one or other brand, one could

Above: February 16, 1944. The truck/trailer alignment was the same when the 1-ton was towed by a cargo dump, as seen here at Ordnance Depot O637 near Bristol, England. (U.S. Army SC-295226)

Middle: 1941, South Carolina during land-air exercises. A cargo YP-G-4112-YJ Chevrolet from the 65th Observation Group has just refueled. (Private collection)

Left: A cover rack model No 2. Various improvements punctuated the production of these trailers, amongst which was the implementation of drop-sides to allow for easier access without having to remove the whole canvas. (U.S. Army SC-145301)

Above: A K-51 with its K-52 trailer. The spare wheel has been relocated under the trailer as its bracket has been was removed to make room for outer storage on the right side and the rigid pipe running along the tiller to protect the electric cable that feeds the radio equipment. (U.S. Army SC-42-MP-1374)

Below: October 15, 1941, Signal Corps Laboratories, Fort Monmouth, New Jersey. This SCR-299 radio set—inside a rare Chevrolet panel delivery ZP-G-4105-ZG, only 149 units of which were produced—is operational and towing a 1-ton trailer K-52. (U.S. Army SCL-179)

Right: Somewhere in New Guinea, a K-51 and K-52 at work. The generator's ventilation was ensured by opening the sides and back of the canvas, the exhaust pipe passing under the floor and to the rear of the vehicle to dispel noxious fumes. (U.S. Army SC-182759)

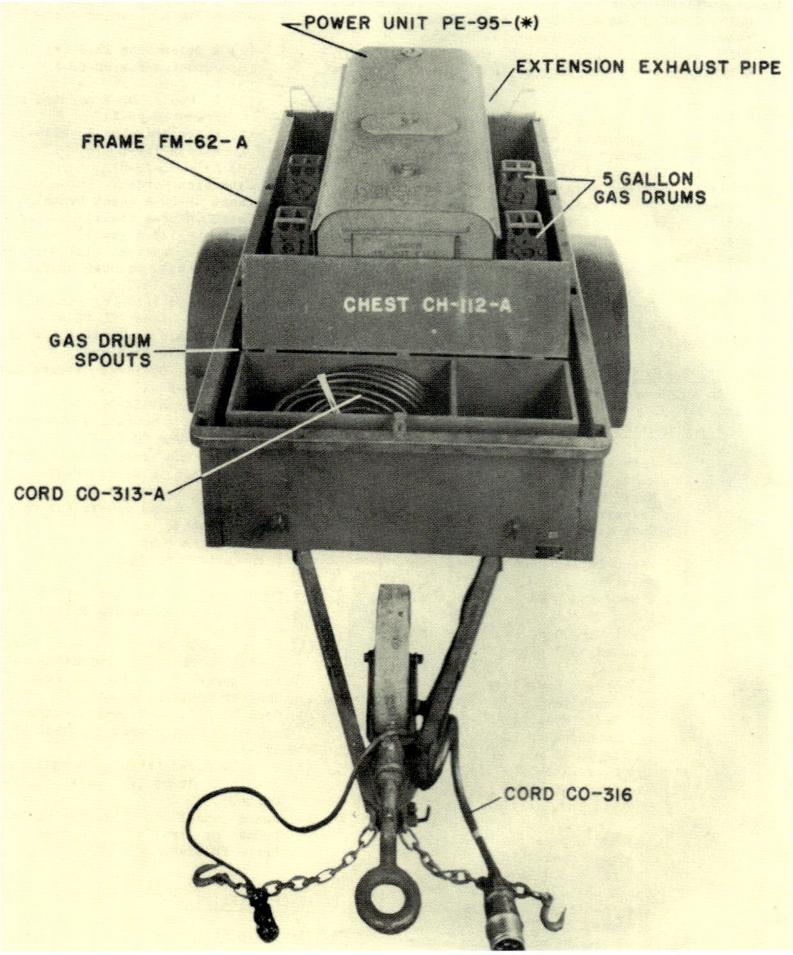

Below: The 1-ton trailer was transformed by the Signal Corps into a K-52 trailer. Equipped with a PE-95 generator and various accessories, it completed the Chevrolet panel delivery K-51. (Photo TM 11-281)

differentiate a square or a round axle, different sizes for the handbrake where the arm was as high as the trailer or similar to the ¼-ton trailer's, or even the same handbrake located at the rear right or at the front right of the chassis.

During production, two elements were adapted to suit strategic necessities: whilst the plain stand quickly made place for a wheel with tire and inner tube, in order to save on rubber, it was equally quickly replaced with an all-metal wheel, either soldered or riveted, some records even making mention of a spoked wheel.

The main body, which required a lot of steel, was replaced in 1942 by a wooden structure, this configuration appearing around June 1943 after stocks of steel bodies were depleted. Finally, by the end of 1944, the shortage of steel not being as severe, the fragile and hard-to-maintain wood was again replaced by steel.

Design

The steel version had a self-supporting body with integrated chassis, and the wooden one wooden panels fixed on a steel frame, with both versions being connected to the axle by two leaf springs. The swiveled tow hook was attached, along with the spare wheel, to a double-rod tiller. The electric installation connected to the towing vehicle was the traditional military type, with the blackout mode triggered by a switch at the rear left of the trailer (this was not present on the earlier production models). Equipped with three

Another Pacific island, this K-51 and K-52 belong to the 60th Signal Battalion, with nothing quite like local vegetation to provide camouflage. Note that the rigid pipe which protected the electric cables on the first K-52s has made way for a simple flexible line affixed to the trailer body. (U.S. Army Signal Corps)

removable drop-sides and four arches, the 1-ton trailer was protected by an integral canvas attached to 12 anchor points by small cords (full rings on the metal version, hooks on the wooden one). To facilitate the use of this cover, each angle was secured with two leather straps.

This early Chevrolet G-7105-NG model is not equipped with the blackout drive and still displays the factory protection on the phone cable reels. It is heading to the Chicago Field Museum, to join the military communication section's collection, covering the Civil War and the two world wars. (Private collection)

13 On Campaign

The systematic abandonment of the smaller 1½-ton, 4x4 in favor of the 2½-ton, 6x6 line, without cancelation of orders or allocation numbers, freed up many Chevys for a multitude of sometimes surprising uses.

As the saying goes, "Nothing is lost, nothing is created, everything is transformed" and Chevy users demonstrated a striking ingenuity in making the most of their rides.

Below: Chaplain John P. Ginter of the 8th Infantry Division, August 18, 1941, Fort Jackson, reads the sermon from a 1-ton public address van trailer. (ACME ATL616519)

Below: The 1-ton, 2-wheel public address van trailer was used not only as accommodation and an office for the chaplain, and the transport of his belongings, but also as a confessional. (U.S. Army SC-118752)

Fort Sam Houston, Texas, June 1941. Chaplain Charles M. Kinard from the 2nd Infantry Division poses in front of his mobile chapel. This model, a panel delivery YP-G-4112-YG, demonstrates perfectly the flexibility of the Chevrolet line. The van could take the equipment necessary for holding a service in front of at least 2,000 G.I.s, including full sound system, a generator, a record player, microphones, and a tent (which can be seen in the background). Setup was done by the unit receiving the chaplain. (U.S. Army SC-118753)

An early ALG A-1 control tower. Despite camouflage nets, this winchless Chevrolet G-7107-NJ's shape is readily identifiable, including the structure of its cargo frame and the removable observation dome. (U.S. Army Air Forces)

Above: Normandy, Saint-Pierre-du-Mont, the evening of June 8, 1944. The Advanced Landing Ground A-1 is waiting for the first P-47s of the 366th Fighter Group. The 834th Aviation Engineers Battalion of the Ninth Air Force are setting up. Note the Dodge ambulance and two Chevrolet cargo trucks, one used as a control tower, while the other with the jerry cans as a telephone exchange. The Harley-Davidsons are General Elwood R. Quesada's escort from IX Fighter Command. (U.S. Army Air Forces)

In the weeks following the Allied landings, several dozen airfields were prepared. The control towers were home-made and installed on vehicles. Seen here is another G-7107-NJ, nicknamed "Butch" and with a pinup on the door. Its registration number X-32616 indicates a vehicle that has been repaired, rebuilt, or possibly returned by the British. (U.S. Army Air Forces A-16355)

Right: The RAF base at Ridgewell, England, November 10, 1944. This G-7117-NM cargo truck with winch has a registration number USA-393091-S. Mounting a small turret on the cabin with a stand for an M32 12.7-mm machine gun was usually meant for a GMC CCKW, but as both cabins were similar, it was a simple enough task for the men of the 381st Bombardment Group, Eighth Air Force, to implement. The Chevy is accompanied by a non-identifiable Jeep with its registration number USA-X-25292-S at the base of the windshield. (U.S. Army Air Forces 66158-AC)

Left: The Ordnance Department could supply nine different types of toolkits at a unit's request, the most well-known being lot No. 7 or Wrecker Set No. 7. It included a lifting gantry to be installed in the cargo frame and a standard tow bar. Created in 1937, the gantry was not made for a specific vehicle; it was only in 1940 that its installation was programmed in the long-wheelbase 2½ton, 6x6's body. But smaller units that were not allocated vehicles bigger than 1½ tons did not have a problem with using the 4x4 Chevy as a tow truck. The photograph, taken in 1942, shows a YP-G-4112-YM towing a broken-down Willys Jeep. (U.S. Army SC-163322)

Left: Another example of a Wrecker Set No. 7 in a Chevrolet 4x4. In order to make the most of the truck, it was also used as a mobile campaign workshop: Also evident is Air Equipment Set No. 3 compressor, used mostly to inflate tires but also for spraying and pressure lubrication. On the left is a small ½-ton, 4x4 Dodge WC panel and on the right the back of a ½-ton, 4x4 Dodge VC cargo. (U.S. Army Signal Corps)

Below: Registration numbers USA-W-327770 and USA-W-327982 apply to these winchless YP-G-4112-YH dumps taken from order W-398-QM-8278, both received in 1941. The first is carrying a squad tools set. These vehicles were commonly used in Cavalry and Engineers units for transport of equipment. (Private Collection)

Right: Naples, December 12, 1944. The Health Service mainly used the Dodge WC-54 ambulance for transporting the wounded. However, here is a winchless Chevrolet cargo, whose doors, cabin, and bumper bear the Red Cross. (U.S. Army Signal Corps)

Below: Brownsville Army Airfield, Texas. Registration number USA-3103697 is stenciled on the rear doors of this panel delivery identifiable as a G-7105-NG, issued in 1942 with contract W-398-QM-10912. Freshly out of the Signal Corps' workshops, this K-51's phone cable reels still have the protective covering from the factory. A makeshift platform has been set up as a control tower and observation post for an instructor training P-39 Airacobra pilots. (U.S. Army Air Forces)

Fort Sam Houston, Texas, this Chevrolet G-7107-NJ registered W-350954 belongs to the same unit. The scaffolding allows cameramen to get some height for their shots. Nicknamed "newsreel unit truck," it was mostly used to record news. (U.S. Army SC-176815)

Left: Camp Robinson, Arkansas November 26, 1941. The 162nd Signal Photographic Company has set up a tower for its ZP-G 4163-ZM-registered W-334985. (US Army SC-133782)

Below: July 1941, 1st Cavalry Division maneuvers, Fort Bliss, Texas. The 1st Signal Troop uses a 1½-ton, 4x4 Chevy as a telephone exchange. Radio communications were not as yet standard. (U.S. Army SC-126448)

Above: Setting up a campaign phone line in New Jersey. In 1941, the Signal Corps was widely allocated Chevys, which met their mission requirements. An RL-26 double reel unit is set up in the truck, that allows for a controlled un/winding of the cable. (U.S. Army SC-120539)

Right: This Chevy cargo is a mobile campaign kitchen. The width of the body is enough to fit three M-1937 field ranges, cookers that worked with petrol burners. To increase the work surface, the crew has turned the drop-side seat around on the outside of the vehicle to create shelving. (U.S. Army SC-123365)

14 Planned Obsolescence?

The favorite line of the U.S. Army during the late 1930s and early 1940s, the 1½ tons were quickly replaced by the new 2½-ton generation.

Apart from a few exceptions, the 1½-ton, 4x4 Chevrolet progressively disappeared from the inventory tables of frontline units, to make way for the 2½-ton, 6x6 CCKW.

But explaining this change by the simple replacement of one line for another would be overly superficial. Certainly, it is necessary to consider the Chevy's smaller payload compared to the CCKW, or even the fact that a triple-axle-based mechanical element was

Right: Fort Benning, January 20, 1942. Whether a G-7107 or as seen here a G-4112, the winchless cargo Chevrolet was replaced by the CCKW-353-A1 with Split axles and by the CCKW-353-A2 with Banjo axles. Although similar in appearance, these two models were completely different. (U.S. Army SC-132248)

Below: October 24, 1941, North Carolina. A relaxing day on maneuvers. Some men from the 1st and 36th Infantry Divisions, First US Army, have been allowed a liberty run to Greensboro with their 1½- and 2½-tonners. (U.S. Army SC-130672)

Right: It was not easy to differentiate between a Split CCKW-353-A1 and a Banjo CCKW-353-A2. Apart from the registration number, the only difference was the shape of the wheel hubs. (U.S. Army SC-127233)

Below: From the design of the body's sides, the radiator grille, and the engine compartment, to the fuel tank location and the setup of the battery well, everything was different in the two vehicles. (U.S. Army Signal Corps)

better than a chassis mounted on two axles, but further explanation is needed

Firstly, we must consider a double parameter of production. The capacity of the Chevrolet factories was inferior to that of General Motors Truck & Coach. Furthermore, supplying the vehicles for Defense Aid and Lend-Lease reduced the U.S. Army's production by 43.5 percent. It was therefore completely understandable that the U.S. strategy should focus on a more promising supply. This was not a problem for General Motors as whichever product was favored, they all came from the same stable; for them it was a simple matter of income transfer.

The CCKW line also came in two different chassis: 164-inch long wheelbase and 145-inch short wheelbase. Note the difference in the logos: with General Motors a small plaque was affixed to the grille, whilst Chevrolet stamped its logo on the sides of the engine compartment. (U.S. Army Signal Corps)

Cargo Trucks with Winch

Left: The G-7117, the Chevrolet cargo with winch, was in direct competition with the Split CCKW-353-B1 and the Banjo CCKW-353-B2, both of them equipped with a winch. (U.S. Army Signal Corps)

Centre: Holabird Quartermaster Depot, November 10, 1941, these G.I.s are taking possession of their new 2½-ton, 6x6. (U.S. Army SC-125962)

Below, left: The winch was the same on both GMC and Chevy models: same manufacturer, same model, and same power (10,000 lb), and although the motors were different—GMC 4,418cc, 103 hp, 2,750 rpm vs. Chevrolet 3860cc, 92 hp, 3,100 rpm—performance was near identical. (U.S. Army Signal Corps)

Below, right: Long or short wheelbase, the mechanical components were the same on the CCKW-353 and 352. The first was a beast of burden meant for transport and the other, thanks to its squatter design and its twin wheels, was meant as a traction vehicle. The 352 found its place in artillery units either to tow howitzers or other trucks. (U.S. Army Signal Corps)

Right: January 20, 1942, Fort Benning. This Chevy belonging to the 161st Signal Photographic Company is a G-7105-NG. The Chevrolet panel delivery proved too small for Signal Corps equipment. Once again, the solution was the GMC CCKW-353 K-60. (U.S. Army SC-120534)

K-70 Panel Delivery Trucks

Above and right: The K-60 was used in many ways by the Signal Corps as its large enclosed body allowed a range of options: sound studio, photo lab, workshop, transport of sensitive or fragile materials, radar station control post, etc. (U.S. Army Signal Corps)

K-51 Panel Delivery Trucks

Left: Awkward due to its bulk, costly and not rugged, the K-51 had a limited range and limited uses. It was progressively replaced by an alternative mounted on the General Motors CCKW-353. (U.S. Army Signal Corps)

2nd Armored Signal Battalion at the Desert Training Center, November 21, 1942. The use of the carrying vehicle had a double advantage, as it could be used in its primary function (transport) as soon as the Shelter HQ-17 was in place. In case of a mechanical fault, the radio could also easily be set up on another GMC CCKW-353. (U.S. Army SC-168178)

Signal Corps General Development Laboratory, October 1, 1942. A Chevrolet cab over engine G-4103-YN installing a Shelter HQ-17 via its lifting gear. The solution adopted for replacing the K-51 was a shelter caisson that could easily be set up on a CCKW cargo platform, or even an amphibious DUKW. (US Army SC-172150)

Left: Just as with the Chevy K-51, the Signal Corps radio equipment of the Shelter HQ-17 was powered by a PE-95 generator in a 1-ton trailer K-52. (U.S. Army Signal Corps)

Winchless Cargo Dump Trucks

Common service vehicles in cavalry units, the cargo dumps without winch were later allocated to the Corps of Engineers and quickly relegated to sideline tasks. (U.S. Army SC-162466)

The Chevy was most of all a victim of its design and the enormous demand for all-wheel-drive trucks on a worldwide scale. As powerful as it was, the U.S. industry had its limits and overall, it was the need for some specific components, like axles, that exacerbated the crisis. The Timken-Detroit Axle Company, main manufacturer of Split-type machinery was suffocating under too high a demand. Alternative solutions had to be found as the purchase orders for 2½-ton, 6x6s kept on coming.

The U.S. Army fleet had several hundred CCKW-352 cargos. Gallion Company took care of transforming the standard short cargo frames into dumpsters with cabin protection. (U.S. Army Air Forces 68700 A.C.)

Left: The CCKW line also had a winchless cargo dump, the L1 model, but very few replaced the Chevy. Only 1,300 were ordered, all equipped with a canvas roof. (General Motors 23800-71)

Cargo Dump Trucks with Winch

Middle left: The Chevrolet 1½-ton, 4x4 cargo dump G-4112-YL, G-4162-ZL, and G-7116-NL were all replaced with CCKW-353-H1s and H2s. The Chevys were not very popular, with only 5,938 units ordered; the winch was there as a precaution. However, the CCKW-353 equipped with the same winch became indispensable during operations, and around 48,000 were ordered. (U.S. Army Signal Corps)

General Motors didn't have to dwell on it for long: compensating for Timken-Detroit's problems was a simple matter of redirecting orders and adapting the Banjo axle production, that equipped the 1½-ton, 4x4 Chevrolet to fit the 2½-ton, 6x6 CCKW. These were the more minor details that precipitated the end of the small Chevy. Straight away the CCKW line grew and had to adopt the 1½-ton Chevrolet's mantle.

Below: The CCKW-352-H1 and H2 had two functions: cargo was for the transport of men and equipment, hence the drop-sides converting to seats; dump was for the transport of loose materials requiring the tilting of the trailer to unload. Two manufacturers shared the task of producing the dumpsters, Heil-Milwaukee and Gar Wood Industries. (General Motors)

Angaur Island, Carolina Archipelago, December 2, 1944, men from the 864th Bombardment Squadron preparing a raid with 1,000-lb. bombs. Although it remained in service throughout the conflict, the bomb service M6 could not keep pace with increasing bombing capacities. Larger-capacity vehicles became necessary. (U.S. Army Air Forces 64099 A.C.)

Left: March 1945, 1st Commando Group Base, India. Unlike the M6, the M27/27B1s were completely mechanized, with a power takeoff on the truck's transmission. The complex web of cables was controlled by levers behind the cabin, at the back of the cargo. (U.S. Army Air Forces 72734 A.C.)

Below: Once more the CCKW-353 brought a solution to the problem with the bomb service M27 & M27B1. There weren't many differences between the two models. The first was equipped with Gar Wood parts, the second with Ernest Holmes Company's. Early in production, the M27 had a wooden body frame; later it was changed to a composite wood/metal; the M27B1 always had a composite body. (General Motors)

15 Lend-Lease

In December 1946, thousands of items that the U.S. had delivered to the Allies as part of the Lend-Lease agreement were listed over nearly 1,500 pages.

Amongst this incredible mass of matériel, 67,613 1½-ton, 4x4 Chevrolet trucks were evident, as well as 238 specific semi-trailers.

All this started when, with the invasion of Poland in September 1939, Europe saw itself once again facing difficult choices. Only too aware of how things ended in 1918, France and Great Britain declared war on Germany. As for the U.S., the Neutrality Act of 1935 had imposed an embargo on the export of military equipment.

Two factions appeared, the hard-core neutralists, and those who would help yesterday's allies. Under Roosevelt's impulsion, a compromise was reached that authorized France and Great Britain to buy equipment, paying cash and on-site. This agreement, called Cash and Carry, commenced in November 1939.

After France's defeat, the British took over the existing French orders, but were soon at risk of being unable to pay. Another helping hand from Roosevelt was needed in order to carry on supporting the Old Country.

Above: A Russian Chevrolet patrolling the ruins of Berlin in 1945. It was one of the 60,475 Chevys of this type supplied to the U.S.S.R. (Private Collection)

Left: The Middle East is not always dry, as these British soldiers and their cargo have discovered. 2,731 vehicles of this type (with or without winch) were supplied to Great Britain. Note the modifications to the lights, as well as the installation of a roof hatch above the co-driver's seat, as was often the case with British machines. (British Ministry of Information E.27586)

May 1943, near El Alamein, this Chevrolet supplied to the British Army has been transformed into a mobile chapel. (U.S. Army Air Forces 80626.A.C.)

On March 11, 1941 and after a few modifications, the Lend-Lease agreement was signed, initially with the United Kingdom and later on with the U.S.S.R., China and a multitude of other nations.

At the outset, when it was only about assisting a few countries, the War Ministry dealt with these transactions on purchase orders by referring to them as D.A. (Defense Aid), but with the increasing number of nations joining the program, Lend-Lease orders were submerged within the U.S. Army's own.

The table below indicates the allocation of the 1½-ton, 4x4 Chevrolet vehicles to the beneficiary countries.

LEND-LEASE 1½-TON CHEVROLET DELIVERIES

Type	Total	U.K.	U.S.S.R..	France	China	Brazil	Latin America	Canada	Netherlands	Misc.
Short Cargo with or without winch	66,340	2,731	60,475	137	16	1,470	451[1]	-	134	926[2]
Long Cargo	52	50	-	-	-	2	-	-	-	-
Dump with or without winch	669	610	-	59	-	-	-	-	-	-
Winchless Bare Chassis	20	-	20	-	-	-	-	-	-	-
Panel Delivery	180	180	-	-	-	-	-	-	-	-
Tractor Truck	49	-	-	49	-	-	-	-	-	-
Bomb Service M6	85	6	-	36	-	38	5	-	-	-
Telephone K-43	133	60	-	73	-	-	-	-	-	-
Auger K-44	35	19	-	16	-	-	-	-	-	-
Fire Truck Class 110	110	30	30	-	-	-	-	-	-	-
Fire Truck Class 135	20	4	-	-	16	-	-	-	-	-
67,613 vehicles were supplied for the Lend-Lease agreement, which represented 43.53 percent of the total production										
Semi-Trailer Stake & Platform	4	-	-	4	-	-	-	-	-	-
Semi-Trailer Van	7	-	-	7	-	-	-	-	-	-
Bomb Trailer M5	191	-	-	134	-	48	9	-	-	-
Trailer K-36	16	-	-	16	-	-	-	-	-	-
Trailer K-37	20	-	-	18	-	-	-	2[3]	-	-

Notes:

1. The 451 cargo trucks supplied to Latin America were split as: 48 to Chile, 72 to Colombia, 2 to Costa Rica, 8 to Cuba, 16 to the Dominican Republic, 30 to Salvador, 14 to Haiti, 34 to Mexico, 20 to Nicaragua, 100 to Paraguay, 13 to Peru, 50 to Uruguay, and 44 to Venezuela

2. Amongst these 926 cargo trucks, 452 were supplied to U.S. government agencies and 474 to smaller Allied countries: 450 to Iran, 4 to Norway, 10 to Poland, and 10 to Turkey

3. Two K-37 trailers were supplied to Canada for research and comparison purposes

Left: For ease of shipping, a large majority of the Lend-Lease Chevrolets were supplied unmounted in crates. Assembly lines were set up on arrival, as seen here in the Middle East. (British Official Photo BM.10244)

Below: Men from the 98th Bombardment Group attend Mass (the same truck seen in the previous photograph). In wartime, religion was a powerful comfort to the troops, whatever the nationality or denomination of the priest. (U.S. Army Air Forces 80624.A.C.)

Above: In Iran, despite the presence of American advisers, the assembly lines for Soviet-destined vehicles remained rudimentary. Employees were mostly from deprived areas, who came to work, sometimes without shoes. (U.S. Office of War Information 29934)

Left: A pile of Chevrolet cargo body frames. On site, Iranian workers kept warm as best they could. (U.S. Office of War Information 29941)

Below: Iran, Master Sergeant Nichola Chekmorath, U.S. liaison officer, with his Red Army counterpart. With some 60,499 Chevrolet 1½-ton, 4x4s received, Russia received almost 90 percent of the Lend-Lease vehicles in this category, and 39 percent of the total production. This is one of the reasons why the line never adopted the canvas roof, as it was disliked by Russian drivers. (U.S. Office of War Information 29931)

16 After the War

It is not easy to work out what became of the 1½-ton, 4x4 Chevrolet after the war. However, a good number of them ended up in the hands of enthusiasts who restored them and gave them a new lease of life.

After the war and disregarding the trucks that were delivered as part of the Lend-Lease agreement, this format of vehicle became obsolete in the U.S. Army, which now focused on ¾-, 2½-, and 4-ton, either in 4x4 or 6x6. Towards the end of 1945 and early 1946, the Army started rationalizing its fleet and anything that was not of use was assembled in huge depots all over the world. The 1½-ton, 4x4 Chevrolet was declassified in large numbers, and only the bare minimum was kept, mostly the auger and telephone maintenance versions to ensure that existing installations could be serviced; it also kept its fire trucks even if they were out of date. A small quantity of cargo vehicles was allocated to the units serving on various military facilities, where the 2½-tonners were too large and the ¾-tonners too small.

What saved some of these Chevys was their full metal cabin because, having modified all other types to help with sea transport, there were almost no trucks left that could protect its riders against the elements. The Russian users, who refused canvas roofs, helped spare their Chevys the open cab conversion and kept it in active service, though of course we are talking of a very limited number of machines compared to the tens of thousands that were in stock.

They were offered with little success to various countries as part of the Western Allies' rearmament program, before being put up for sale. In order to

Kipapa Airfield, Oahu Island, Hawaii. More than 20,000 vehicles were stocked here by March 1946, of which 5,300 Chevrolet cargos were awaiting sale by the War Assets Administration. (U.S. Army CPA-46-1325)

Left: September 1945, a surviving 1½-ton, 4x4 Chevrolet being used as a gauge during tests of the Boeing C-97. The first official C-97 flight took place in 1947. The insignia on the door tells us this truck belongs to the 8th Service Command. (Associated Press Photo 19647C)

Above: The same vehicle, but inside the aircraft hold, which seems to have been made to measure. (Wide World Photo A-51803)

dispose of large numbers of vehicles of all kinds, everything was listed on vast schedules which became the basis for a worldwide auction, organized as close as possible to the various surplus stockpiles by the War Assets Administration.

Covering thousands of pages, each machine was cataloged as a specific lot, defined by its nomenclature, the name of manufacturer, its chassis number and even its registration number. At the end date of the auction process, envelopes were opened, and the highest bidder was named tenderer, after which they had to honor their purchase and ship the machines as soon as possible

Below: Fresh from army stocks and repainted, these Chevrolet cargos joined the ranks of the Ramsey County Post Office, Minnesota, on May 24, 1946, which, in a stroke, updated its delivery fleet. (Private collection)

Because the civilian vehicle industry had long been put on hold, many smaller companies were in search of vehicles, especially ones of the Chevrolet's size. Mechanics converted them into tow trucks, and a host of other businesses found a use for them too, such as bakeries, dairies, and the like. Some larger companies rejigged their entire fleet in this manner to ensure uninterrupted services.

All this contributed to the many Chevys that can still be found today waiting for a new lease of life.

Right: Another example, among so many, Navy Base 16's official milkman has built a protective body on the frame of a Chevy cargo dump. (Private collection)

Below: Chevys were very robust vehicles. This Class 110 was still in service with the Multnomah County Fire Brigade, Oregon, in November 1980, and in its original configuration. (Private collection)

After a brilliant military career and a plethora of services rendered to civilians, these small 4x4 trucks were forgotten.

Left to rust on the side of a dirt track in the country, at the back of a barn or a scrapyard, many Chevy trucks weathered time and elements, sometimes becoming barely recognizable wrecks. Luckily a good deal of them were rescued by enthusiastic mechanics, or automobile history aficionados, often people who are deeply respectful of their duties of remembrance. Dismantled to the last bolt, renovated, rebuilt and restored, they now drive proudly on the highways and byways.

Right and below: Certainly, the most difficult 1½-ton, 4x4 Chevrolet to restore due to its missing, very specific trailer, this G-7113-NK tractor appears old fashioned. It is towing a Winter-Weiss Model S-32-WB 3½-ton combination S&P semi-trailer. The all-wood structure of the trailer is another challenge in the preservation of this model. (Th. Mahot)

Two Chevrolet panel G-7105-NGs, the first in a K-51 radio vehicle configuration, and the second a K-70. They are identical, apart from the fact that one went through the Signal Corps workshops for its radio communication equipment. (Private collection)

A winchless Chevrolet cargo G-7107-NJ followed by a panel G-7105-NG K-51. The attention to detail by these enthusiasts can be seen in the colors of the star and hood markings, dependent on the year of production. (Private collection)

Standardization made differentiating between the various models difficult. The level of restoration of these vehicles is so good, almost identical to a 1940s' lineup. From left: two winchless Chevy cargo G-7107-NJs, a tractor truck G-7113-NK, a winchless cargo G-7107-NJ, a cargo with winch G-7117-NM, a panel G-7105-NG in a K-51 configuration, a G-7105-NG in a K-70 configuration, and a cargo with winch G-7117-NM. (Private collection)

Above: This G-7105-NG K-70's radiator grille is from the first series; made of a median vertical rod and two side coils, this vehicle is not equipped with the blackout drive. (Private collection)

Below: A winchless Chevrolet cargo with the third-series grille, including the protective protrusion on the left for the blackout drive. (Private collection)

Above: This panel K-51 displays a second-series grille; made with vertical rods, it is also not equipped with the blackout drive. (Private collection)

Below: A winchless Chevrolet cargo G-7107-NJ. Its grille has been modified with the in-unit installation of a blackout drive. (Private collection)

Appendices

SPECIFICATIONS

Vehicle	Length (in)	Width (in)	Max height (in)	Min height (in)	Wheel base (in)	Net weight (lb)	Gross weight (lb)	Crew	Max speed (mph)	Fuel tank capacity (gal)	Cruising range (mi)	Fuel consumption (mpg)	Towing capacity (lb)
Winchless Cargo	224	86	107	87	145	7,550	10,875	2	48	30	270	9	4,000
Cargo with winch	231	86	107	87	145	8,223	11,546	2	48	30	270	9	4,000
Long winchless Cargo	286	96	108	87	175	8,973	11,976	2	48	30	270	9	4,000
Panel Delivery K-70	221	87	91	91	145	6,766	10,088	2	48	30	270	9	4,000
Panel Delivery K-51	221	87	95	85	145	7,474	10,796	2	48	30	270	9	4,000
Winchless Cargo Dump	224	86	108	87	145	8,373	11,696	2	48	30	270	9	4,000
Cargo Dump with winch	230	86	108	87	145	9,019	12,341	2	48	30	270	9	4,000
Tractor Truck	206	86	87	87	145	6,032	10,895	2	48	30	180	6	4,000
Bomb Service M6	220	72	92	92	125	6,045	8,384	5	50	40	250	6.25	4,000
Telephone Maintenance K-42	212	90	104	104	145	11,052	11,374	2	48	35	315	9	4,000
Telephone Maintenance K-43	212	90	104	104	145	12,189	12,511	2	48	35	315	9	4,000
Telephone Earth Borer K-44	228	90	104	104	145	10,225	11,561	2	48	35	315	9	4,000
Turret Trainer E-5	216	88	107	87	145	6,781	9,784	2	48	35	315	9	4,000
Field Lighting J-3	233	86	137	137	145			2	48	30	195	6.5	4,000
Field Lighting J-4	233	86	137	137	145			2	48	30	195	6.5	4,000
Field Lighting J-5	233	86	137	137	145			2	48	30	195	6.5	4,000
Fire Truck Class 110	237	88	98	98	145	9,008	12,509	5	48	30	270	14.5	0
Fire Truck Class 135	253	88	97	87	145	9,079	14,013	6	48	30	270	14.5	0
Fire Truck Class 300	245	89	112	112	145	8,662	13,243	6	48	30	270	14.5	0
Fire Truck Class 325	248	89	112	112	145	9,579	14,947	6	48	30	270	14.5	0
Fire Truck Class 525	248	89	112	112	145	9,579	14,947	6	48	30	270	14.5	0
Cab over Engine short Cargo	286	98	99	99	175	8,578	11,900	2	43	30	240	8	4,000
Cab over Engine long Cargo	326	98	142	99	175	8,898	12,220	2	43	30	240	8	4,000
Lowboy	219	102	99	67	137	12,886	15,889	2	50	60	300	5	4,000
Trailers													
Semi-Trailer Van 3- & 3½-ton	220	86	132	132	162	5,805	11,810	2,259 units received					
Semi-Trailer CS&P 3½-ton	201	84	89	47	148	4,586	11,592	1,959 units received					
Bomb Trailer M5	217	94	44	44	102	2,202	7,207	16,212 units received					
Bomb Lift M22	122	56	58	42		1,803	6,810	4,037 units received					
Trailer K-36	122	72	68	56	72	1,817	6,821						
Trailer K-37	146	91	68	69	117	2,903	12,912						
1-ton Trailer	140	72	73		100	1,283	3,324	259,064 units received					
Semi-Trailer K-55	295	95	115	115	215	8,208	12,712	125 units received					
Bomb Lift M1								20,310 units received					

SEMI-TRAILERS REGISTRATION NUMBERS Van Semi-trailer, 3- & 3½-ton (6-ton gross), 2-wheel				
Manufacturer	**Type**	**Year**	**Units**	**Registration numbers**
Fruehauf Trailer Co.	Model 118-S	1940	9	04440 to 04448
Highway Trailer Co.	Model SKD-2043 Model SKD-1742A	1942 1941	5 206	054814 to 054818 (Special Chemical Warfare Service) 054819 to 054896 et 056258 to 056385
Checker Cab Mfg Co.	Model CC-3	1942	191	065057 to 065243 et 0101635 to 0101638
Carolina Truck & Trailer Co.	Model M-2-A	1942/3	955	0158048 to 0158197 + 0316282 to 0316425 + 0377370 + 0485290 to 0485389 + 0633877 to 0633945 + 0657716
Black Diamond Trailer Co	Model T-118 Van	1943	373	73 taken from series 0310359 to 0310523 + 0633643 to 0633701 + 0656339 to 0656579
Kingham Trailer Co.	Model H-30-S Van	1943	50	Taken from series 0314459 to 0314608
Steel Products Co.	Model BSV	1943	301	0316426 to 0316725 + 0658207
Strick Co.	Model 300 Van	1943	56	Taken from series 0319266 to 0319465
Truck Engineering Corp.	Model 2-SF Van	1943	150	Taken from series 0324890 to 0324890
			2,296 ordered by the U.S. Army of which 2,259 units received	
Combination Stake and Platform (CS&P) Semitrailer, 3½-ton (6-ton gross), 2-wheel				
Dorsey Bros	Model D-8	1941	201	014311 to 014361 + 0192624 to 0192773
Highway Trailer Co.	Model 18-3-SB	1941	6	014380 to 014385
Winter-Weiss Co.	Model S-32-W	1941/2	420	039312 to 039401 + 043293 to 043337 + 047484 to 047540 + 056125 to 056241 + 056502 to 056612
Checker Cab Mfg Co.	Model CC-4	1942	224	065244 to 065467
Strick Co.	Model 300	1942/3	477	144 taken from series 0319266 to 0319465 + 0141827 to 0141861 + 0668818 to 0669115
Krieger Steel Section Inc	Model KEF-1116	1942	17	0141862 to 0141878
Black Diamond Trailer Co.	Model T-118	1942/3	116	92 taken from series 0310359 to 0310523 + 0141879 to 0141902
Kingham Trailer Co.	Model H-30-S	1942/3	150	100 taken from series 0314459 to 0314608 + 0141903 to 0141952
Utility Trailer Mfg Co.	Model G-SW-2	1942	64	0141953 to 0142016
Truck Engineering Corp.	Model 2-SF	1943	143	2 taken from series 0324890 to 0324890 and 141 with no registration numbers
			1,818 units ordered by the U.S. Army	
Van Semi-trailer Model K-55, 1½-ton, 4-wheel				
A.J. Miller Co.		1942	98	090804 to 090808 + 0102824 to 0102916
Oneonta Linn Corp.		1942	27	0100506 to 0100512 and 20 with no registration numbers
			125 units ordered by the U.S. Army	

TRAILER 1-TON, 2-WHEEL CARGO REGISTRATION NUMBERS				
Manufacturer	**Type**	**Year**	**Units**	**Registration numbers**
American Bantam Car Co.	Model T-6	1943	27,000	0399083 to 0417082 + 0592113 to 0601112 (8,4131)
Baker War trl	Model T-6	1945	2,271	0868388 to 0870658
Ben-Hur Mfg Co.	Models 41-120 & 41-33	1942–5	66,053	0108343 to 0116432 + 0116437 to 0123346 + 0174769 to 0176371 + 0129362 to 0129884 + 0137768 to 0138417 + 0424772 to 0449431 + 0605438 to 0612637 + 0658208 to 0668817 + 0860688 to 0863687 + 0974824 to 0975219 + 01106063 to 01107582 + (16,0971)
Checker Cab Mfg Co.	Model CC-5	1942	5,500	0123362 to 0128361 + 0128862 to 0129361
Checker Cab Mfg Co.	Model CC-5A	1943/4	48,345	0295583 to 0310358 + 0361124 to 0377047 + 0614965 to 0621989 + 0706570 to 0717189 (15,8821)
Century Boat Co.	Model T-6	1943–5	2,533	0518711 to 0519910 + 0613765 to 0614964 + 0992630 to 0992762 (1,2001)
Covered Wagon trailer		1945	126	0994357 to 0994482
Dorsey Bros	Model T-6	1943	2,000	0543322 to 0544321 + 0637936 to 0638935 (6881)
Gerstenslager Co.	Model A	1943	29,500	taken from series 0325742 to 0355741
Gerstenslager Co.	Model A	1943/4	31,865	0575500 to 0592112 + 0669116 to 0683467 + 0722159 to 0723058 (20,9531)
Henney Motor Co.	Model H1	1943	4,450	0505023 to 0506772 + 0509273 to 0510472 + 0603013 to 0604512 (1,5001)
Hercules Body Co. Inc	Model T-6	1943–5	6,989	0527511 to 0530110 + 0863688 to 0866187 + 0941356 to 0943242
Highland Body & Trailer Co.	Model T-6	1943	2,750	0524711 to 0527460 (5081)
Hobbs Mfg Co.	Model O-901-D	1943–5	5,677	0500273 to 0503272 + 0602063 to 0603012 + 0982315 to 0984041 (1,5091)
Hyde Trailer Co.	Model L-1	1944	950	0601113 to 0602062 (9401)
Keystone Trailer Co.		1945	65	0866188 to 0866252
Lavine Gear trailer	Model 41-33	1940/1	10,458	09031 to 014238 + 039511 to 043006 + 043044 to 043047 + 043540 to 045289
Mifflinburg Body Co.	Model T-6	1943	1,388	0515823 to 0517210 (3361)
Nabors Co.	Model 3GC	1943	1,500	0510473 to 0511972 (454 not accepted)
Nash Kelvinator Corp	Model A	1941/2	44,628	024139 to 039138 + 049711 to 054710 + 059395 to 061394 + 069186 to 090785 + 1,028 with no registration number
Olson Mfg Co.		1943	1,200	0509273 to 0510472 (1,2001)
Omaha Standard Body Co.	Model TW-1	1943	2,675	0503273 to 0505022 + 0604513 to 0605437 (1,4071)
Pike Trailer Co.	Model T-6	1943	2,000	0519911 to 0521910 (781)
Queen City Mfg Co.	Model T-6	1943	2,800	0521911 to 0524710 (3641)
Redman Trailer Co.	Model T-6	1943	3,000	0614990 to 0616489 + 0517211 to 0518710 (1,5001)
Steel Products Co.	Model AC	1943	3,500	0541322 to 0541821 + 0541822 to 0543321 + 0544322 to 0545821 (1,4981)
Streich & Bros Co.		1940	6	unknown registration
Strick Co.	Model US	1943	2,500	0506773 to 0509272 (1,0141)
Transportation Equip Co.	Model T-6	1943	1,500	0539822 to 0541321
Truck Engineering Corp.	Model T-6	1943	3,100	0512723 to 0515822
Willys-Overland Motors Inc	Model TW-6	1943	18,000	0381083 to 0399082 (3,2241)
Winter-Weiss Co.	Model T-6	1943	3,500	0496773 to 0500272
			337,829 units ordered by the U.S. Army	
1. Not received. Only 259,064 units were received				

Bibliography

Technical Sources

Technical Manual TM 9-760, Bomb Trailer M5, 08/22/1942
TM 9-762, Lift Truck M22, 05/31/1943
TM 9-765, Bomb Service Truck M6 (Chevrolet), 08/13/1942
TM 9-805, 1½-Ton, 4x4, Truck (Chevrolet), 12/30/1943
TM 9-883, 1-Ton, 2-Wheel Cargo and Water Trailers, 08/27/1943
TM 9-1765A, Axles, Propeller Shafts, and Wheels for Bomb Service Truck M6 and 1½-Ton, 4x4, Truck, 03/02/1945
SNL-G-85/G-506, Truck 1½-Ton, 4x4 (SNL G-506) & Truck Bomb Service M6 (SNL G-85 Vol. IV), 06/25/1945
TM 10-1127, Chevrolet 1½-Ton (LC) 4x4 Trucks Models G-7105, G-7106, G-7107, G-7713, G-7116, G7117, G-7127, and G-7133, 06/10/1941
TM 10-1127 Ch.2, Chevrolet 1½-Ton (LC) 4x4 Trucks Models G-7105, G-7106, G-7107, G-7713, G-7116, G7117, G-7127, and G-7133, 03/01/1942
TM 10-1131, Chevrolet 1½-Ton (LC) 4x4 Trucks Cab Over Engine Model G-7123, 1941
TM 10-1203 Ch.4, Chevrolet 1½-Ton (LC) 4x4 Trucks Models G-7163, and G-7173, 03/01/1942
TM 10-1430, Chevrolet 1½-Ton (4x4) Trucks Models G-4105, G-4113, G-4152, G-4162, G-4163, G-4165, and G-4174, 06/15/1941
TM 10-1431, Chevrolet 1½-Ton (4x4) Trucks Models G-4105, G-4113, G-4152, G-4162, G-4163, G-4165, and G-4174, 1941
TM 10-1438, Chevrolet 1½-Ton (4x4) Trucks Models G-7105, G-7106, G-7116, G-7107, G-7117, 03/02/1942

The same lineup of Chevrolet trucks as the image on page 154, viewed from the other side; note the differences in development between the radiator grilles and headlamps. (Private collection)

TM 10-1461, Chevrolet 1½-Ton (LC) 4x4 Trucks Model G-7105, 04/01/1942
TM 10-1557 (Ch.1), Chevrolet 1½-Ton (4x4) Trucks Models G-7105, G-7106, G-7107, G-7713, G-7116, G7117, G-7163, and G-7173, 07/07/1942
TM 9-2700, Principles of Automotive Vehicles, 11/18/1947
TM 9-2800, Standard Military Motor vehicles, 09/01/1943
TM 9-2800, Military Vehicles, 10/1947
TM 9-2800-1, Military Vehicles, 09/1953
TM 5-270, Standard Stream Crossing Equipment, 11/01/1940
TM 5-687, Fire-Protection, Equipment and Appliances, 01/1946
TM 11-227, Radio Communication Equipment, 04/10/1944
TM 11-364, Truck K-44-B and Earth Borer, Equipment HD, 09/24/1942

Publications

Summary Report of Acceptances, Tank-Automotive Material, 1940–1945. Chief of Ordnance, Detroit 1945
Ordnance Department, Administrative and Tactical Vehicles, 1940–1944. Automotive Center 01/01/1944
Ordnance Department, Administrative and Tactical Vehicles, 1940–1945. Automotive Center 10/01/1945
Engineering of Transport Vehicles, 1942–1945. Chief of Ordnance, Detroit 1945
Lend-Lease Shipments World War II. Office of the Chief of Finance, War Department, 12/31/1946
Chevrolet Trucks, Vehicles of Victory. Portrayal Press
Standard Catalog of US Military Vehicles. David Doyle, Krause Publications, 2003
US Military Wheeled Vehicles. Fred W. Crismon, Crestline Publishing